ACHIEVE YOUR DREAMS

MICHAEL "Truth" MOORE

Dedication

I dedicate this book to my father,

the greatest man I have ever known.

Acknowledgments

To my wife

Natalie, and my son MJ who are

my inspirations

Table of Contents

Introduction

...You've been misled

You've been had.

You've been took.

-MALCOLM X

Do you want to reach your full potential in life? There is more success and wealth than you can imagine waiting for you. It is yours for the taking. You have the skills, the intelligence and the passion to achieve great things. Deep down, you know this to be true. You know you are capable of so much more. But if you are like most African Americans, you feel like something is holding you back. You feel like something gets in the way of you getting what you want. But what is it?

First, you must understand the truth as to why you do not have all the successes you desire right now. Whether it is in the form of money, weight loss, healthy relationships, booming business or family life. The truth is that your current results are not caused by some force outside of yourself as most people believe. There is no "boogeyman" that tries to stop you every time you try to achieve something. The truth is your results are caused by your "mental conditioning" about who you are and what you are capable of doing.

One of the secrets to being successful is understanding that your behavior is causing your current results; both positive and negative. And the "way you think" is causing your behavior. But if your "mental conditioning" is so important to your success, where did it come from?

It comes from a variety of places such as your parents, family and friends. Primarily, it comes from Society. Society teaches your parents what to teach you when you are growing up. Psychologist call this "Social Conditioning." This process is used to teach you how to act and what to think about yourself. One of the interests of this book will be to reveal how society has tricked you into believing negative things about yourself. These negative beliefs are the primary reason why you struggle to reach your full potential. As a Black person, you have many unique challenges in your life and this book is written specifically to help you overcome them. My goal is to help you achieve the results you want.

Let's play a game to see the effects of "Social Conditioning" in action! Let's pretend for a minute that you are a white person living in America. In this case, society teaches you a rich history full of success and opportunity. In your history class, you learn that you come from great explorers like Christopher Columbus and share the same skin pigment with Benjamin Franklin and Abraham Lincoln. You are told that you are capable of doing great things: You are a descendant from great businessmen, scientists and inventors like Ford, Einstein and Edison. "With just a little hard work and ingenuity, you can be anything you want to be". These are all positive messages and sound empowering, don't they? But the problem with this game is that you are not a white person.

You are a Black person and the society's message to you is much more destructive to your psyche. Society's message to you is that you come from slavery. That your people were owned and sold like animals at a large market. "You are mentally inferior. You have a lower IQ. You are unattractive because of the color of your skin. You are inherently prone to be a criminal, lazy, promiscuous and destructive"...and the list goes on and on.

To demonstrate the effects of this type of negative messaging on children, let's create an imaginary friend. Let's say our friend's name is Becky. Becky is a very happy 12 year old white girl living in America.

One day, Becky is whisked away to an island called "Blacktopia." On this island, all the people are wealthy and successful Black people. In Becky's school, she is taught that she is not as smart as Black people because she is white. She is taught that her long blonde hair is stringy, doglike and dirty. She is told that her pale skin is unattractive and disgusting. After being taught these things for several years, how successful and happy do you think little Becky would be when she grows up? Not very successful or happy because her mindset would be based on a negative view of herself.

As a Black person, this is the same type of negative propaganda that keeps bombarding your mind every second of your life. Just like Becky, what chance do you have of being successful and happy if you think this badly about yourself? Not a very good chance at all. This is why it is so important to change your mindset about what it is to be a Black person before you set off to accomplish your life goals.

But most of us simply try to ignore these negative stereotypes because we feel like we can't change them. In order to change them, we would have to change the way the world views Black people and that is not possible, right? So our solution is to ignore the problem. But ignoring the problem does not work either, so what are you to do? After reading this book, you will know what to do to solve this problem.

The first step is to acknowledge that this is really happening and it is a real problem in your life. You must accept the fact that you have been systematically taught and indoctrinated to believe in

Black inferiority since birth. Even if you reject it on a conscious level, you have definitely been forced to believe it on a subconscious level.

For example, I remember one day sitting in class. I was the only Black person in the class with 25 white students. The teacher said, "today we are going to read Huckleberry Finn." Each student would read a page in front of the class. I had never heard of the book but the cover had a black person on it, so I was excited to read it.

One of the white students started reading out loud and immediately I heard "Nigger Jim did this...Nigger Jim did that." In case you have never read the book, "Nigger Jim" is Huckleberry Finn's friend who is a runaway slave. The teacher told me the book was written by Mark Twain and is one of the greatest American novels ever written. How does hearing white kids call a black man "Nigger Jim" over and over help my self-esteem as a black person? Needless to say, I hated the book.

The book taught the class some very negative things about Black people. It taught the white kids that they were better than me because I was Black. It also taught me that I was helpless and stupid just like "Nigger Jim" because I was Black. Society shapes everyone's opinion about black people in a harmful and destructive way.

This negative conditioning is not just something that happens when you are taught in history class as a child, it is drilled into your subconscious mind as an adult as well. It is perpetuated by the media and society as you get older. When you see movies like 12 years a slave, Django Unchained, The Help and the likes, you are continually reminded that you are a product of slavery. A spawn of a shameful past who is inherently inferior to white people: Which is absolutely not true. One of the first things I will teach you is to never support media or messages that portray you as inferior and a second-class citizen. This is an unacceptable behavior that must not be found in any Black person who wants to be a winner.

Winners do not let people talk down on them. Winners do not dwell on past defeat. Winners do not let others dictate their reality. Winners focus on improving every day. Winners focus on their future successes.

Do you really think Michael Jordan or his fans sit around and watch clips of all the games he lost? No, they watch highlights of his amazing winning games? Winners always focus on the positives and propel themselves forward towards achieving more success. This is what winners do and this is exactly what you will learn to do.

You can't develop a winner's mindset by sitting on your couch watching black people act like slaves on TV. Do you think you will be in your best frame of mind to go on a job interview after watching some white slave-owner rape a black woman on TV? Of course not.

While all these propaganda are pure poison for the Black mind, it is a powerful potion that stirs the white mind. You see, the white man is afflicted with a disease called jealousy. The propaganda he uses to keep you down is actually the antidote he created for his own insecurities. He has always been, and continues to be, intensely jealous of Black people like you.

The white man is jealous; of the way you look, the rhythm in which you move, the creativity of your mind, the way your skin glistens in the sun. His jealousy is undeniable. So much so that he nearly kills himself each summer trying to get a tan to look just like you. White women get butt implants and lip fillers to look like Black women.

But the thing that makes him the most jealous is the scientific fact that God created Black people first. White scientists have proven, with extensive evidence that all mankind looked just like you in the beginning. Ponder on the different types of people on earth; Europeans, Asians, Arabs, Indians, Jews, etc. All these people are just genetic mutations derived from the Black man and Black woman. This fact is what drives the white man crazy; the fact that he was not the first. How do you think he feels with the knowledge that all humanity started with you? That the one true God of all creation chose to make you first and not him. It is important for you to understand this so that you can understand what motivates him to constantly attack you. You must learn to adjust your mindset in order to deal with this reality. Their jealousy and greed has always been the root of their contempt for Black people.

I learned this lesson first hand when I was 11 years old. On a bright summer day, a group of friends and I were playing touch football in front of my house. There were 10 kids playing and I was the only black person on the field. I was happy, laughing and smiling that day. Life was good. In one game, I had scored 4 touchdowns and we were beating the other team badly.

To put it bluntly, I was better than my friends at football. I could run faster, jump higher and catch the football better than they could. On one particular play, the ball was thrown to me high into the end zone and I had to jump as high as I could to catch it. Andy, the kid defending me, was my good friend and he jumped to keep me from catching the ball. I jumped over him and snatched the ball from his hands for a touchdown. In the process of catching the ball, I came crashing down on his shoulders and forced him to the concrete. Andy fell hard and skinned up his knee pretty bad. I landed on my feet, towering over him with the ball in my hand. It was a proud moment for me so I spiked the football and did my best 'end zone dance'.

Now keep in mind, Andy and I had been friends our entire lives. I hung out at his house with his family once or twice a week and we had never had a disagreement before let alone an argument. But on this day, our friendship changed forever.

After I scored my touchdown, Andy stood from the ground and pushed me hard from behind. My body lunged forward and I did my best not to fall down. I turned around and smiled, thinking he was just playing or something. Maybe he was even congratulating me. But he was not playing and he definitely was not happy that I scored the touchdown. His face was a furious bright red, his knee was bleeding and he was pissed off. By this time, all the other kids had surrounded us in a circle as if they were expecting us to fight. Since Andy was my good friend, I had no intention of fighting him over a meaningless football game. I thought I would just apologize for hurting his knee and everything would be fine. Not this time.

Andy ran over to me, planted himself right in my face and says, "you think you're so good at everything don't you?...Well, you ain't shit." I replied..."calm down. It is just a game. It's not like I cheated or something. Why are you so upset?"

Andy says, "I know you think you're better than me but my dad told me something about you. He told me I will always be better than you. I replied..."You're crazy. You are not better than me." His voice got louder, "Yes I am. I know I am. My dad told me so. He told me that my great grandfather owned your great grandfather and treated him like a filthy animal. That's all you are to me is a filthy animal, you f*in Nigger."

Wow. Never in a million years would I have thought Andy would say something that evil to me. I was shocked. My blood began to boil and I could feel rage well up inside of me. At the same time, this was happening and the kids in the crowd started chanting something at the top of their lungs. Their faces were lit up with joy and laughter. They chanted, "A fight. A fight. A Nigger and a White. If the White don't win, we all jump in." They said it so happily over and over again. I stood there in disbelief, my heart racing and head pounding. I thought to myself, "These are my friends. Why are they chanting such racist stuff? What have I ever done to them?"

By this time, Andy was fuming and staring me right in the eyes. He pushed me again. At this point, I wish I could tell you that I kept my cool: I wish I could tell you that I turned the other cheek and walked away. I wish I could tell you that I debated with him in a rational manner about the importance of good race relations. Unfortunately, I can't tell you that. I was an angry and enraged 11 years old who was seething with a furious face. I was blinded by anger and before I knew it, my hands had swollen into fists and everything went into slow motion. The next thing I knew, my fists were raining blow after blow down upon his face. His nose began to spray blood all over my shirt. I just kept hitting him over and over again in a blind rage until someone finally pulled me off him.

The worst part about the entire experience was not what he said. Rather, it was that I actually thought he could be telling the truth. I began thinking to myself..."Is his dad right? Did his great grandfather really own my great grandfather? Had he done some research and discovered something I didn't know about my family history? Am I just a savage brute that fights the moment someone calls me a name? Why am I so angry at being called a Nigger? Why can't I just call him a Nigger and then we would be even? What is a Nigger anyway? I was confused. My mind dizzied with troubling thoughts. Why was this happening to me?

This is how the negativity of racism and propaganda damages the minds of our little kids. It makes them think something is wrong with them: That they are the cause of the problem or that they are always overreacting in some way. But this is not true.

Just like Andy, when the white man looks at you, he sees greatness and he is jealous of you. This makes him begin to use every medium to teach you to see yourself as a failure in order to keep you down. Have you ever sat back and wondered..."why do some white people hate black people so much?" You see it on the news all the time. A police officer kills an unarmed black person for no reason like in the Eric Garner case. Trayvon Martin was gunned down in cold blood for wearing a hoodie and walking home in his own neighborhood. What about the college students at UCLA who took photos in blackface to make fun of Black people. What did you ever do to them that makes them want to expose you to such cruelty, hate and racism? I will tell you what you did. You were born with greatness inside you and they are jealous of that: That is the sin for which they condemn you.

They have spent the last 500 years trying to shackle, demoralize and beat that greatness out of you but they haven't been able to achieve that and the same cycle happens in every generation. They recognize that greatness within you; it's time you recognize it as well. Enlightened Black people are the ones who understand their history and recognize the game that is being played in order to rise to the top. It happened during slavery and it is happening now. That is why you are reading this book. You are seeking enlightenment! You know that there is more in store for your life. More satisfaction. More happiness. More wealth. More love. People like you are destined to rise to the top.

In order for you to rise to the top, you have to understand that white superiority is a lie. This is important because you live in America and you are being bombarded with messages that support this belief. The idea that white people are better than you because they are white, is a concept this country is breastfeeding on. You can't just ignore racism and focus on your goals while thinking you will achieve them. Unfortunately, it's not that easy: You have to confront it. You have to master it. You have to dismantle it in your mind so that you can reach your goals. You must know in your soul that white superiority is a lie.

Sometimes when you see the wealth that the white man has, you think that he must be extremely smart to have gotten it. And since you don't have his wealth, you think you are not as smart as he is. This is a logical way to think but it is also a 'logical' lie which I will prove it to you.

I know white people well. I have dated their daughters. I have played sports with their sons. I have had fist fights with their cousins. I have spent summers in their homes. I have cried with them at funerals. I know them well indeed and after spending decades in their world, I have learned some things that I would like to share with you.

The parents of my white friends were doctors, lawyers and politicians. Some of my white friends have grown up to be CEO's of major corporations that employ thousands of people. These people are the elite. They are blue blood that attend private high schools and Ivy League colleges like Harvard and Yale and in my many years of living with them and talking to them, I can tell you one plain fact that you probably won't believe. They are not special! They have as many problems, anxieties, addictions and fears as Black people do.

Now don't get me wrong. Some of them have brilliant minds and others have more money than they could ever spend. They have all the material things you could ever hope for in life. But not one of them is inherently great or superior to you. More importantly, they know this to be true. That is why they are so hell-bent on keeping you oppressed.

What they do have is a tool called "white privilege." What that means is their ancestors did some really evil things to obtain wealth and power, and now their descendants are benefiting from it.

Please get me right: I'm not saying that white people don't work hard and don't have any real accomplishments, because they do. However, just like any enterprise or business, resources like money and time that are invested earlier into it remains the thing that matters. That's where the big money is made. The early money and resources invested is the factor that created billions of dollars for people like Bill Gates and Mark Zuckerberg. Well, in the case of the American enterprise, the early money was put up by Black people. Blacks invested billions of dollars in free labor which took the form of slavery. Business people call this "sweat equity". Blacks were the early investors that got the American economic engine off the ground. The major problem that is facing you is that Black people did not get the huge payoff from their efforts. It was stolen from them; stolen from you! Wouldn't it be nice to have been given a million dollar trust fund that was passed down to you by your great-great grandfather when you were born? Of course it would. But unlike your white counterpart, you do not have generational inheritance and wealth passed down to you.

Keep in mind that labor is always one of the most expensive line items in a business. Imagine if IBM, GE or Microsoft just stopped paying all their employees for the next 300 years. Don't you think their path to winning would be much easier? Of course it would.

Why does this matter to you? It matters because not understanding this concept will keep you brainwashed into thinking that the white man's wealth comes from his intelligence or greatness. His wealth has nothing to do with either. He stole his wealth from the early Black investors in the form of slavery.

Imagine if I robbed a bank tomorrow for fifty million dollars and I give the money to my 20 year old son. Let's say he then buys himself a mansion in Beverly Hills and several exotic cars. One day you will see him on television talking about how wonderful his mansion is and then conclude that he must be a very intelligent person to have so much wealth at such a young age. This seems like a logical pattern to think, doesn't it? In fact, you might feel like he is smarter than you because he has much more than you do. But in fact, he is just "privileged" to have a daddy who robbed a bank. Once you understand how he got his wealth, you would stop thinking he is smart and hardworking. Because he is not.

The idea is that you should stop seeing what white people have and thinking that they are somehow smarter than you because they have wealth. To get that wealth, they killed nearly all the American Indians and enslaved millions of Africans for nearly 500 years. There is nothing to be proud of there or to aspire too.

The next time you see a white guy at your job driving an expensive car or building a huge house. Don't sit there and attribute what he has to his intelligence or determination. When you do that, you put yourself in a position to feel less than him and that is not the case. It is better to attribute it to his white privilege because that is the truth as to the reason he is in the position that he is in. White privilege has bestowed him with generational inheritances such as houses, and estates that are passed down. White privilege ensures that he has the opportunities available so that his hard work and perseverance have a chance to pay off for him.

I hope your eyes are beginning to open because I want you to see the reality that I see. I see a race of Black people who are only 50 years into integration and are trying to compete with a race of white people who have had a 500-year head start. Even with this massive head start, the racist laws, past lynching, and cops murdering our kids, we are catching up in all areas of society. How great and famous do you have to be in order to close such a huge gap quickly? The greatest! This is why you should not see yourself as less than. Rather, see yourself as more than.

The reality of what we are accomplishing as a race is astonishing. We have put a Black man in the White House. We dominate all the major sports and entertainment. We have done all these in such a short period of time that it is unbelievable. The last hurdle left for us is to dominate the educational and business sector; we are beginning to move in that direction. People like you who are reading this book, and embracing my message of Black empowerment, are the leading the charge. Once you are mentally empowered, you can accomplish your life goals. You can start a business, go back to school, lose weight, write your book, get that promotion, buy the house you always wanted etc. All it takes is for you to believe in yourself and accept the understanding that you are an offspring of the greatest people on earth. This greatness that you possess is what scares the white man to death. He knows if you start to focus on how great you are, there is no force on earth that can hold you back.

This is why he works so hard to keep you focused on the negative. If he truly believed that you were inferior he would not waste his time and money to keep you down, right? You would not even be a threat to him if you were truly inferior. Do you think a Gazelle spends any time thinking about what an ant will do? Of course not, because the ant poses no threat. But that same Gazelle will spend his entire life worrying about the action that the lion will take. You're the lion and the sooner you realize that, the sooner you will step out of fear into your destiny.

The system of mental oppression started centuries ago and continues to this day. You have been taught generation after generation that everything about Black people is bad. From the shape of your nose to the color of your skin. You are even taught to associate the color black with darkness and pure evil. No matter how much success you have had in your life, this propaganda has affected you. It is holding you back from reaching your God-given potential. My mission is to help you break free and achieve your life goals.

The only thing you need is a positive belief in your own greatness. That's it. Once you stop believing "this is just the way life is" or "it's never going to change", you will begin to attract success. Everything you need to achieve greatness and change your life is already inside of you. A swift acceptance of this truth is important in order for you to become the person you have always wanted to be.

Now that you understand that your mental condition is the cause of your current behavior and results, you are ready to take a journey with me towards reaching your destiny. You must decide with every ounce of your being to eradicate all the negative stereotypes that society has taught you about yourself and Black people in general.

This is because you have subconsciously internalized so much negativity about being Black that you cannot break free without a considerable amount of work. To make the necessary alterations in this area does not only takes time but it also takes a respectable amount of study and discipline. However, it is worth it!

It is well worth every ounce of energy you can muster. You will learn how to undo the harmful mental programming that has been passed down and installed within you.

This book will take you on an exciting journey that will create a new you. You will be reborn with the same body but with a more

POWERFUL mind. A mind free of fear, limiting stereotypes and boundaries. A mind capable of ACHIEVING whatever goal you set.

When you read this book, read it as if I were a personal friend writing to you. This book is now dedicated to you as I want you to succeed at whatever your goals are. Read it again and again as you develop your new mindset. Underline sentences, memorize quotations, and highlight words that are meaningful to you. Complete the exercises in this book until you master them.

Call on this book often, as it will bring newer meanings as you grow in your personal life. With each reading, you will uncover what lies behind each concept. After you have digested all the ideas, put them into action! You will know beyond a shadow of a doubt that there is no reason for you to be held back any longer. Make your choice to be the greatest you possible!

Free Your Mind

In performing this task, one must ask what it means to be brainwashed. A person who is brainwashed is one that has internalized the negative things that do not fit in with reality. For the black person, it means removing every negative stereotype about their culture which causes him to boil with self-hatred and low self-esteem. In the case of people like this, associating with the white man is the only means of escaping the sin of being born black.

The black community experiences a challenge which is the non-observance and little celebration of the successes we have achieved and this is due to self-hatred. When they have been brainwashed to think that their contributions to humanity are worthless, why won't they keep hating their efforts. Unfortunately, the self-hatred has caused many Black people to think lowly of themselves and also find ways of destroying their fellow black people who may be trying to succeed in any enterprise they set up.

Let us look at some easy ways to find out if you are being mind controlled:

1. Brainwashed Black people believe they must add "Indian blood" or any other blood when describing their family line because they have low self-esteem.

2. Brainwashed black people think that successful black men like NBA stars mostly end up getting married to white

women when in reality, 86% of them are married to beautiful bold black women.

   a. Brainwashed Blacks are often fond of attributing their heritage to the Caribbean instead of Africa which is the historic original birthplace of Black people.

3. Brainwashed Blacks often think that the whiteness of the skin is the reason why white people seem to have better prospects in life and think that white people are super geniuses.

4. Brainwashed Blacks often find themselves believing in stupid statistic that claim that white-owned businesses treat customers better as opposed to black-owned businesses. In most cases, such brainwashed folks do not ever visit Black business sites to confirm or refute such rumors.

5. Brainwashed Blacks are often fond of calling every light-skinned woman pretty because of their skin and long hair. They do not often pass such courtesy to dark-skinned women.

6. Brainwashed Blacks of the worst kind are those that believe that long hair that is flowing and silky belongs to the best class while those which are curly and kinky are terrible.

7. Brainwashed Blacks believe that laziness is a distinct feature of a black man and that is why the black people have more people on welfare than white people.

Fortunately, this statistics is very incorrect as 2011 U.S. census showed that White people are on welfare more than Black people.

8. Brainwashed Blacks often make off-handed use of clichés such as, 'black people are like crabs in a barell as they always pull one another down when any of them tries to escape". The brainwashed Black would say that Blacks cannot be trusted with anything. And they forget that trust is a human virtue that does not belong to any exclusive racial group.

9. Brainwashed Blacks are those who are easily gullible. They are the ones that believe the news propaganda that maintains that the population of black people in jail is much more in comparison with white prisoners. The U.S. Prisons statistics of 2011 actually showed that there were about the same amount of white people in jail as black people.

The Trickery of the Racist

Propaganda goes by numerous other synonyms like indoctrination, brainwash etc. but the general idea behind it is that it is a form of communication that is projected in a way that influences the attitude of a particular community towards a cause. It is usually perfected by the subtle art of presenting only one side of an argument. Propaganda is so deadly a tool that it is used on different media in order to bring the required changes which it hopes to achieve within the audience who have no idea what is going on

Have you ever read the book, 'Eighteen Ninety-four' by George Orwell? It was set in a society where the government was a big brother that controlled the minds of the citizens using every means possible.

In the case of Black people, it is a wonder how much we often do not see racist agenda being applied in the creation, justification and maintenance of the heavy oppression that the Blacks are often subjected to.

The Aims of Racism.

There is a very important TV documentary created by Marlon Riggs which you should watch. 'Ethnic Notions' is the name of the revealing flick and it is a brilliant attempt that shows the pathway taken by White America in thoroughly degrading the Black image and mental state. I think you should know that there is a lot of money being spent in keeping you down and your peculiar racist experiences are not accidental as the media will want you to believe. The question is that, "To what end is Racism targeted?"

The reason why it is very much in full force is that there is still the jealousy held by the White man towards the Black man. He wants you to think of him as being superior and dominant to you just like Charles Darwin pictured in his book, Origin of Species, where he ranked the Negroid stock at the bottom of the races.

The White man fears the successes achieved by the Black man and wants to still hold on to the material resources which he has gotten from previous generations. They want you to have nothing and not take the lead in any form of human activity and that is why they try to brainwash Blacks to believe that we are subpar in every form of human expression and activities like beauty, intelligence, skills, body physique, health, moral dispositions, passion etc.

Racism would have you believe that Black people have wild emotions which they are incapable of taming while White people are reserved and better in their passion and the purpose of this is to justify the negative treatment of Black people. It is also a medium that is used to ensure that resources and opportunities are set aside for the White population while the Black population are not given any reasonable resources. They try and show that Blacks are more crime-prone in order to justify their excessive use of force but it is a lie that keeps damaging the Black community.

How Is Propaganda Used Against Blacks?

Human beings are naturally selfish beings who cringe when they are being put under someone or anything. This meant that in the historical relationship between the Whites and Blacks, force was the tool used in order for the Whites to get us to work for them for free. In using horrifying means of coercion such as brainwashing and social conditioning, they convince us to feel bad about our natural selves.

The second method which is less violent and deadlier was developed over the course of more than a century and solidified by numerous White professionals. Even though it took longer, the method of brainwashing and social conditioning has shown itself to be more effective. According to Carter G. Woodson in his work, Miseducation of the Negro:

If you can control a man's thinking you do not have to worry about his action. When you determine what a man shall think you do not have to concern yourself about what he will do. If you make a man feel that he is inferior, you do not have to compel him to accept an inferior status, for he will seek it himself. If you make a man think that he is justly an outcast, you do not have to order him to the back door. He will go without being told; and if there is no back door, his very nature will demand one and cut one to enter.

Stop Supporting A Harmful Media

Marches have always been a tool which have ensured the presence of change through the years. In the case of the movie premiere of the film 12 years a Slave, many people from the audience walked out in order to register their distaste at gruesome scenes of slavery where slaves were tortured and killed. Harvey Weinstein who was the Toronto movie studio chief made mention of the fact that many African American movies were being shown at the festival because of the 'Obama effect' as it served as a reawakening of Black films on the major screens.

While it is a joyful delight for everyone to see brown faces on major screens after so much time spent in the shadows, we may want to ask some important questions. The first of such questions is that, Are the Black movies really representative of our original experience or fakes aimed at perpetuating the subtle aim of social conditioning?

This question becomes glaring when we identify one major fault in most Black movies. Most of these movies are usually set against a backdrop of slavery, torture and chaos and the question that we ought to ask is that "Is this the only struggle that characterizes the story of the Black man?" We should be forced to ask why we are portrayed as bloodthirsty and why our history is shown to begin in slavery and not the great civilizations of Africa such as the empires of Songhai, Mali, Ife, Kingdoms like the Great Zimbabwe, Benin, Buganda which were vast in size and majestic in the height of their glories.

12 Years A Slave and movies like it are the slow poison that is toxic to our children. Do you really think a 9 year old girl needs to see another Black child being beaten and called a Nigger in a movie? This poison seeps in through the introduction of "Blackness" during the so-called Black History Month where our children are shown video clips and taught lessons that instill in them the thinking that our history begins at slavery and ends just before the fight for civil rights. They learn that this country has hated them before they were born. Then, they are secretly trained year after year to believe that something is wrong with them because they have brown skin. This is happening every February to you and your children! Do you see how damaging this is to your mind?

I remember sitting in the living room with my parents when I was about 7 years old and everyone gathered to watch the premiere of Alex Haley's "Roots." In case you are not familiar with "Roots", it is a TV mini-series about American slavery. My parents were so excited to watch it. Prior to watching this movie, I always felt powerful as I knew in my mind that I could run faster, jump higher and was smarter in school than my white friends. That was how I honestly felt and I loved the feeling.

Two weeks of watching the "Roots" mini-series, my self-esteem was destroyed. I could not believe the way black people were raped, butchered, hung and murdered in the movie. The positive way I thought about myself and other Black people was shattered and I remember thinking to myself, "why in the hell didn't they just kill those white folks who were enslaving them." Surely that is what any logical person would have done, right?

Even at 7 years old, I knew that a white man could not come into my home and slap my mother. My father would kill that man with his bare hands for even thinking such a thing. My father was a proud and noble man who would do anything to protect his family. That seemed normal to me: that is the American way!

Like many fathers in my neighborhood, my dad had a controlled rage that laid just beneath the surface and that protected our family. How then could the black people in "Roots" not possess the rage to fight against everything that was happening to them? How could they let the white people beat, murder and rape them?

I could not understand it.

I was told they were my ancestors but they did not act like any Black people I had ever met and I became confused and distraught. No child should be subject to this type of negative imagery regardless if it really happened or not. We must protect our children's minds because they are fragile. Those fragile child-like minds, when exposed to such media, grow up to be broken adult minds and that is a real problem.

Those people who try to replace negative images with positive ones immediately hit a brick wall at most times because such gruesome images are very profound in a way that they even form nightmares. Unfortunately, our children continue to be bombarded by such images and when they reach their Black history classes, they most times find themselves feeling inferior in comparison to their white classmates who feel like conquerors.

What we discover is that our kids associate the word "Black" with something degrading, suffering and nothing glorious. They wander around in depressing gait and their emotions become heightened because they expect other races to mistreat them. These negative feelings are often triggered when we begin to pass down racist remarks and insults which were generated during the slavery era. Poets with microphones and writers with their pens ought to be very careful in order to avoid repetitions of these negative past because their works are digested by 3rd graders who would have continued to maintain their innocence and high self-esteem had they not been shown such negative past history through images on film screens or in books.

Your Black history did NOT begin with slavery! Slavery was a significant part of our transition to this country but it is not the most pivotal part of our history. We are no longer slaves. We are no longer bound by anything but our own beliefs. In fact, Black people ruled the world for over 20,000 years. The current White/European rule is only about 600 years long. But you would not know that without knowing your world history.

You owe it to yourself and your family to cut the cord on movies that glorify a historical account that is far removed from your current experience. This attachment to self-victimization is the bane of our entire society. Every race, every face should distant itself from the 'woe is me' mentality that teaches us to define ourselves by the struggles we have passed through.

The people who caused your pain want you to think there is honor in struggling but this is a lie. There is no honor in struggling! There is no honor in being a victim and there is surely no medal in losing. When we define ourselves by the horrific incidents we overcame, we seek to prove our strength yet we are doing quite the opposite. We are actually glorifying our weaknesses and the mistakes that lead to the situation that we needed to overcome: There is no honor in doing that. You should never do that because it is damaging to your self-image.

There is only honor in putting the past mistakes behind you and winning the next fight. The greatest boxer of all time, Muhammad Ali lost to Joe Frasier in a stunning defeat in their first fight. There was no honor for Ali in that loss and no reason for him to talk about that limiting experience or even acknowledge that it happened. He focused on training harder and channeled his efforts towards devising a better strategy so he could win the next time. Ali won their next two fights and his victories brought him honor which they wrote in his obituary when he passed on in 2016. It did not talk about his losses or his mistakes. There were no focus given to those negative events. Rather, it glorified his victories and his contributions to the world.

I want you to remember that there is no honor in your pain and suffering. But there is honor in winning and accomplishing great things. There is honor in going back to school, starting a business and raising a family. Seek honor in your victories not your losses.

Any Black person who tells you how strong Black people are because they suffered through slavery and survived is an Uncle Tom. The person is stating an obvious fact but that fact is not something to be proud of. Like a silly parrot fed with the master's biscuit, he is just repeating what he heard the white man say about Black people's suffering. He doesn't realize that line is being used to demean Black people, not celebrate their strength.

It's like a woman being viciously raped by a man and the man then says, "You are a really tough woman. I brutally raped you over 500 times and you did not even cry once. I'm going to call your parents and tell them they raised a really strong woman. They should be proud of you." That sounds ridiculous, doesn't it? Your only focus should be channeled towards condemning the rapist for his evil actions.

Hey! Don't let the white man tell you to be proud of surviving his brutality. Be proud of the successes that Black people have accomplished in science, business, engineering, athletics, music and world history. Those are the types of things to be proud of.

Let us then rise and give a standing ovation for those moviegoers at Toronto festival who walked out. Let us walk out in solidarity with other moviegoers in the future when we see a misrepresentation of our proud history. Doing so will show that we want stories that will reflect our realities and future pursuits. Stories that showcase the rise of business moguls like Stan Lee, Dr. Dre, and Oprah Winfrey should be showcased in the movies. Movies that tell the ways in which we can rise above the towering mountains in our journey to success should be shown more often. Imagine a movie premiere that centers on President Barack Obama's rise to power and then think of the impact which films such as Hidden figures is currently having on Black kids these days.

Hidden Figures is a film about three Black women who were scientists that rose through the ranks at Ivy League schools that did not accept Blacks. Still, they rose and ultimately were given jobs at NASA where they led the team that ensured the successful landing of the first man on the Moon. Imagine the kind of positive impact which this movie had for Blacks at the cinemas! Boycotting movies like 12 Years A Slave and Django Unchained must become a necessity unless you have a fantasy for seeing people being tortured brutally.

We should take concrete steps to counter the kind of wrong conditioning which the society is doing to our kids. One of such concrete steps is to determine the kind of stories they listen to and watch as these will ultimately help them shape their self-esteem and fuel their pursuits. When we see horrendous Hollywood movies that are intent on dragging them back to an era of mental subjugation which we have tried to come out from, we should immediately stop them. People who revisit their traumas often find themselves going backward, and for Blacks, it means we should stop celebrating those old wounds.

Blacks are not solely products of a painful past. Rather, you should think of what your today looks like. What is your "collective experience"? Is it one that is ruled by fear and paralyzes you while giving you the feeling that you need the white man's permission to move ahead? Do not allow that fear rule you because you need to show your children the best way to move forward. You need to tell them that they can achieve anything with the right mindset. They need to know that they are born great and are the descendants from the first man. Keep repeating the scientific fact that the first man and woman originated from Africa. This means you are God's pure image who is never to end up last.

It is important that we create a new slate for our kids by showing them that the color of their skin is something to be proud of. Thus, we should never support films that keep playing the race cards over again. Affirmative words have always been key to building confidence in kids, and that is why we must speak affirmative words to them.

"You are beautiful" "You are loved". "Nothing can limit you". "No one holds rule over you". "No one has the keys but you".

Tell them of the need to reject negative stereotypes. Tell them that they have the weapon of choice and they should use it to reject every negative image that are used as tools to bring down their self-esteem

People who tend to underestimate the level which negative images affect them often end up at the wrong side of the road and you should avoid this. You should be careful enough to spot out these negative images, as they can be subtle in popular cultures such as music, films, and education and even in some civil rights movement.

Here is the way propaganda works: Black youths are pictured with other Black friends; devising ways to rob other black families and thinking of the best way to sell cocaine in order to show a lavish lifestyle.

Simply put, propaganda begins to pump Blacks with a negative energy and make them feel as though they have to hate each other. So here is a way which we can beat that;

Think of every black person you meet as a dignified king and queen. Condition your mindset to spot out their positive talents and their brilliant minds instead of the 'dumbness' that the media tells you to look out for.

In most occasions, I have tried to paint this scenario for Black people in different areas and I encourage them to overcome self-defeating attitudes like hatred, worshipping of white ideas and the belief that the white man is the excellent one.

It is not shocking that in most cases; people tend to act out the script written by those who oppress them. They are like puppets that do not know what is going on and these are some of the ways they act;

- They think that black films are dumb and white films are so awesome

- They think that Black skin, Hair, lips, body shapes are ugly

- They think that black people are always in a state of chaos and cannot organize

- They believe in the efficacy of a white lawyer getting them out of trouble quicker than a black lawyer

- They always exhibit disrespect to other Blacks but begin to cower when talking to White people

- They disregard Black authorities

- They do not see anything good ever coming from Africa

Great critics of the anti-Black propaganda have emerged through the years and continue to arise with the aim of fighting the system. These brothers like Brother Malcolm X and Amos Wilson, Naim Akbar should be fondly remembered as titans who took on issues like self-hatred, identity crisis and ensured that the Black race understood the need to stick together.

Focus on the Positive

When you listen to the news, you discover that Black people are at the top of every bad statistic and at the bottom of every good statistic. But this is just more propaganda. The media houses are choosing to report the bad and not the good in a bid to keep you in a negative place.

Below are statistics from the several documented sources showing the positive things that are happening in the Black community. Because you have been used to hearing negative statistics, you might not believe these statistics are accurate. But I can assure you that they are.

- 9 out of 10 black people, 12 years or older, currently don't use illicit drugs.

- 93% of black people don't suffer from substance abuse issues.

- 78% of black fathers, ages 15 to 44, who live with their children bathe, dress, diaper, or help their child use the bathroom daily — For white fathers, it is only 73%.

- 9 out of 10 young black adults, ages 25 to 29, have completed high school or its equivalent — the same ratio as the national average.

- Among Boston-area universities and colleges, Tufts, Harvard, MIT, Boston College, Boston University, Bentley, Babson, and Emerson graduates, there are over 80% black men who are enrolled.

- There are nearly 60% more black men in post-secondary educational centers than in jail.

- Black high school graduates are 3 times more likely to be in college or employed than unemployed.

- Black fathers, ages 15 to 44, had the highest rates of helping their children with homework and taking them to and from outside activities than white fathers in the same age group. 78% of Black fathers versus only 72% of white fathers.

- 6 out of 10 black young adults, 25 to 29, have at least some college — the same ratio as the national average.

- Nearly 80% of black fathers living with their children read to them. Only 74% of white fathers read to their children.

SOURCES: US Census, American Council of Education, US Health and Human Services, Centers for Disease Control and Prevention, The Education Trust, NCAA.org, Pew Social Trends

What is the way out?

There is no gain in saying the fact that change is a phenomenon that does not occur easily. A situation wherein change comes for a people who have been downtrodden for centuries will not be easy but there are some practical steps that can be taken to counteract the anti-Black propaganda.

The first step is known as self-realization wherein you recognize the fact that every black person, including yourself, has been brainwashed at one point or another.

Secondly, you have to make it a point of duty to teach the younger generation the way to distinguish between what is true about the Black race and what is propaganda.

In the third step, every effort should be channeled towards the identification and exposure of the White man's attempts to misrepresent the Black race; remember the Toronto walkout.

And lastly, there is nothing more enlightening than reading about our past. Pick up books and read of Africa's past before the coming of the Europeans. Read about the scientific discovery of Africa as the home of civilization, and read Black works that continue to raise the standards in their industries.

Live By A CODE

In 2018, I started an organization called 'Black Achievers.' This is an organization that comprises of the best and brightest Black people from all walks of life. Our members live by a Code that helps them strive for excellence in everything that they do. I would like to share this code with you.

1. Truth

   I am honest with myself and with others.

2. Success

   Anything is possible. I have no limits.

3. Family

   I protect my loved ones at all times.

4. Honor

   I am a person that keeps my word. I do what I say I will do.

5. Spirituality

   I am made in God's image. God is Black like me.

6. Education

   I seek true knowledge and reject all lies.

7. Politics

   I vote for people who support me and the Black community.

8. Media

   I do not support media that is negative towards Black people.

9. Economics

   I financially support my family and the Black community.

10. Unity

   I seek unity with Black people throughout the world.

Know Your History

The following is a **modified excerpt** from a speech given by **Malcolm X** on the importance of knowing your history. Remember, history is NOT what happened, but rather a story ABOUT what happened. American society changes and alters the stories to empower whites and to make you feel weak and inferior. But you must understand this game and the lies that they tell you.

Ancient Black civilizations

The condition that you are in is directly related to your lack of knowledge concerning the history of the Black man. The Black man's history goes back to the beginning of recorded time. Black civilizations ruled the world for over 20,000 years.

Once you do the research, you will find that on the African continent there was always a higher level of culture and civilization, than what existed in Europe at the same time period.

The Sumerians were Black people who ruled the Middle East

At least five thousand years ago, there was a Black civilization in the Middle East called the Sumerians. When they show you pictures of the Sumerians they try and make you think that they were white people. But if you go and read some of the ancient manuscripts, you'll find that the Sumerian civilization was a very dark-skinned African civilization, and it existed in the same area where you find Iraq today. It was a dark-skinned people who lived there, who had a high state of culture way before the Europeans.

The Dravidians were Black people who ruled India

And at a time even before the Sumerians, there was a dark-skinned people living in India, who were also Black called Dravidians. They inhabited the subcontinent of India even before the present people that you see living there today, and they had a high state of culture. The present people of India even looked upon them as gods; most of their statues, if you will notice, have pronounced African features. The religion that they practice is called Buddhism. They give all their Buddhas the image of a Black man, with his lips, his African nose, and even is hair. And these African people lived in that area before the present people of India lived there. This is why current Indians have such a wide range of ethnic skin color.

The Black man also lived in Egypt along the banks of the Nile. And in Carthage in northwest Africa, another part of the continent, and at a later date in Mali and Ghana and Songhai and Moorish civilization—all of these great civilizations existed on the African continent before America was discovered.

The Egyptians were Black people from Africa

Now the Black civilization that amazed the white man the most was the Egyptian civilization, and there is no denying that it was a Black civilization. It was along the banks of the Nile, which runs through the heart of Africa. The white man was so jealous of this African civilization that he tried to convince the world that

Egyptians were European and not African. He wrote books about it, put pictures in those books, make movies for television and the theater—so skillfully to convince other white people that the ancient Egyptians were white people themselves. But they were African and so were the pharaohs of ancient Egypt. Which means that the white man himself, he knows that the Black man had this high civilization in Egypt. He knows that the Black man had mastered mathematics, mastered architecture, the science of building things, had even mastered astronomy.

The great pyramid, as the white scientists admit, is constructed in such a position on this earth to show that the Black people who were the architects of it had a knowledge of geography that was so vast, they knew the exact center of the earth's land mass. Because the base of the pyramid is located in the exact center of the earth's land mass, which could not have been positioned by its architect unless the architect had known that the earth was round and knew how much land there was in all the directions from where he was standing. The pyramid was built so many thousand years ago that they don't even know the exact time it was built, but they do know that the Black people who brought it into existence had mastered the science of building, had mastered the various sciences of the earth, and had mastered astronomy.

When you read the opinions of the white scientists about the pyramids and the building of the pyramids, they don't make any secret at all that they marvel over the scientific ability that was in the possession of those African people back then. They had mastered chemistry to such extent that they could make paints whose color doesn't fade for thousands of years. The white man today hasn't learned how to make paint that will last even two years without fading while these Africans made paints that last 2,000 years. And the Black man in that day was such a master in these various scientific fields that he left behind evidence that his scientific findings exceeded the degree to which the white man here in the West has been able to rise today.

And you must know this, because if you don't know this, you won't really understand what there is about you that makes them so afraid of you, and makes it imperative for them to keep you down, keep you from getting up. Because if they let you up one inch, you'll get up and you're gone to the top of the mountain.

Just behind the pyramids is a huge statue, which many of you are familiar with, called the Sphinx. The people who live over there call it Aboual-Hole, which means "father of everything." This too was put over there so long ago they don't know who did it, nor do they know how long ago it was done. And they marvel at it. What causes them to marvel is the fact that the Black man could have been at such a high level then, and now be where he is today, at the bottom of the heap, with no outer sign that he has any scientific ability left within him. And he himself doesn't believe that he has any of this ability within him; he thinks that he has to turn to the white man for some kind of formula on even how to get his freedom or how to build his house.

But the Black man by nature is a builder, he is scientific by nature, he's mathematical by nature. Rhythm is mathematics, harmony is mathematics. It's balance. And the Black man is inherently balanced. Before you and I came over here, we were so well balanced we could toss something on our head and run with it for miles. You have lost your balance so much that you can't even run with your hat now —you can't keep it on.

You've gotten away from yourself. But when you are in tune with yourself, your very nature has harmony, has rhythm, has mathematics. You don't need anybody to teach you how to build. You can build by yourself. You play music by ear. You dance by how you're feeling. And you used to build the same way. You have it in you to do it. There are brickmasons from the South who have never been to school a day in their life. They throw more bricks together and you don't know how they learned how to do it, but they know how to do it. When you see one of those other people doing it, they had to go to school— somebody had to teach them. But nobody has to teach you...you know how to do it. It just comes to you. That's what makes you dangerous. When you become proud of yourself, a whole lot of other things will start coming to you, and the man knows it.

Europeans were in the dark ages

In that day the Black man in Egypt was wearing silk, he dressed sharp as a tack. And those people up in Europe didn't know what clothes were. They admit this. They were naked or they were wearing skins from animals. If they could get an animal, they would take his hide and throw it around their shoulders to keep warm. But they didn't know how to sew and weave. They didn't have that knowledge in Europe back then.

They didn't cook their food in Europe. Even they admit when they were living up there in caves, they were knocking animals in the head and eating the raw meat. They were eating raw meat, raw food. They still like it raw today. You watch them go in a restaurant, they say, "Give me a steak rare, with the blood dripping off it." And then you run in and say, "Give me one rare too, with the blood dripping off it." You don't do it because that's the way you like it; you're just imitating them, you're copying, you're trying to be like that man. But when you act like yourself, you say, "Make mine well done." You like cooked food because you've been cooking a long time; but they haven't been cooking so long—it wasn't too long ago that they did not know what fire was. This is true.

You were walking erect, upright. You ever watch your walk? Now you're too cool to walk erect. You've come up with some other type of walk. But when you're yourself, you walk with dignity. Wherever you see the Black man, he walks with dignity. The white man have a tendency to be other than with dignity, unless they're trained. When their little white girls go up to these highfalutin schools, and they want to teach them how to walk, they put a book on their head. Isn't that what they do? They teach them how to walk like you. Because you were almost born with a book on your head. You can throw it up there and run with it. When you travel to Africa you will see our people naturally have that poise and that balance. But this is not an accident. This comes from something. And you have it too, but you've been channeling yours in another direction, in a different direction. But when you come to yourself, you'll channel it in the right direction.

Hannibal was an African man that ruled in Europe

There was another African civilization called Carthage. One of the most famous persons in Carthage was a man named Hannibal. You and I have been taught in the movies that he was a white man but he was actually a Black man. This is how they steal your history, they steal your culture, they steal your civilization—just by

Hollywood producing a movie showing a Black man as a white man.

Hannibal was famous for crossing the Alps mountains with elephants. Europeans couldn't go across the Alps on foot by themselves—no, they couldn't. Hannibal was a brilliant general. He found a way to cross the Alps with elephants. You know what elephants are—great big old animals, it's hard to move them down the road. Hannibal moved them across the mountains. Hannibal was a Black man with a brilliant mind.

Why do Italians have such dark complexions?

Hannibal had with him One Hundred Thousand African troops, he defeated Rome, and occupied Italy for nearly twenty years. This is why you find many Italians dark—they got some of that Hannibal blood. No Italian will ever jump up in my face and start talking bad about me, because I know his history. I tell him when you talk about me, you're talking about your pappy, your father. He knows his history, he knows how he got that color. Don't you know that just a handful of Black American troops spent a couple of years in England during World War II and left more brown babies back there—just a handful of Black American soldiers in England, in Paris and in Germany blackened the whole countryside. Now, what do you think one hundred thousand Africans are going to do in Italy for twenty years? It's good to know this because when you know it, you don't have to get a club to fight the man—you can just put the truth on him.

There really are Black Irish people

Even the Irish got a dose of your and my blood when the Spanish Armada was defeated off the coast of Ireland, around the seventeenth century. The Spanish in those days were dark. They were the remnants of the Moors, and they went ashore and settled down in Ireland and right to this very day you've got what's known as the Black Irish. And it's not an accident that they call them Black Irish. If you look at them, they've got dark hair, dark features, and they've got Spanish names—like Eamon De Valera. These names came from the Spanish-Portuguese peninsula, and they came there through these seamen, who were dark Africans in those days. Don't let any Irishman jump up in your face and start telling you about you—why, he's got some of your blood too. You've spread your blood everywhere. If you start to talk to any one of them, I don't care where he is, if you know history, you can put him right in his place. In fact, he'll stay in his place, if he knows that you know your history.

West Africa had high culture

So all of this Carthage, Sumerian, Dravidian, Egyptian, Ethiopian history took place B.C., before Christ. In this era that you and I are living in after Christ, right in West Africa, one of the most highly developed civilizations was Ghana. Ghana wasn't located where she is today geographically, she wasn't limited to that geographic location. She covered pretty much a great portion of West Africa, and it came to power right around the time of the birth of Christ. And it was a highly developed civilization, highly developed society, that prevailed right up until the eleventh century, But this was an empire in Africa that was the source of gold and ivory; and other art objects, what would be called today art objects or items of luxury, came from Ghana. They had one of the most highly developed governmental systems, tax systems and cultures.

Timbuktu was an African city considered the center of knowledge in the world

After Ghana in West Africa, there was another civilization called Mali. Mali is one of the most famous because it was made famous by a Black sultan named Mansa Musa. Mansa Musa was famed for a journey he took from Mali to Mecca. In the same area—all of these three empires were in West Africa—after Mali, it was the Songhai Empire. The Songhai Empire covered even more territory than the Mali Empire. And in those days there was the fabulous, fabled city of Timbuktu.

Timbuktu was a center of learning where they had colleges and universities; and this Timbuktu existed as a hidden city, or forbidden city, to the white man for many centuries. He was not permitted to go there, none of them had been there—it was for us. They had universities there in which scholars traveled from China, Japan, the Orient, from Asia, from Africa, all the parts of Africa, to come there and learn. This was in Africa, and this existed before the discovery of America.

These people who taught at these universities had a knowledge of geography. They knew that the earth was round. It wasn't Columbus that discovered that it was round for people in Europe; they discovered it when they began to be exposed to the science and learning that existed in the universities on the African continent. But the white man is such a liar, he doesn't want it to be known that the Black man was so far ahead of him in science.

Those in power told lies deliberately and scientifically to distort the image of Africa in order to mold a better picture and image of Europe—you can see the crime that they committed once you begin to delve into the African continent today and find its real position in science and civilization in times gone by.

The Moors were African and ruled Europe for 700 yrs.

Also, a little later was a civilization called the Moors. The Moors were also a dark-skinned people on the African continent, who had a highly developed civilization. They were such magnificent warriors that they crossed the Straits of Gibraltar around the year 711, eighth century, conquered what we today know as Portugal, Spain, and southern France, conquered it and ruled it for seven hundred years. And they admit that during this time Europe was in the Dark Ages, meaning darkness, ignorance. And it was the only light spot; the only light of learning, that existed on the European continent at that time were the universities that the Moors had erected in what we today know as Spain and Portugal.

These were African universities that they set up in that area. And they ruled throughout that area, up to a place known as Tours, where they were stopped by a Frenchman known in history as Charles Martel, or Charles the Hammer. He stopped the invasion of the Africans, but the Africans ruled in this part of Europe for over 700 years before they were stopped.

They try to confuse you and me by calling them Moors, so that you and I won't know that they were Africans. But when you go home, look in the dictionary. Look up the word M-o-o-r; it will tell you that Moor means black. But they don't want you to know that we were warriors that we conquered, that we had armies, that we once ruled Europe and most of the world.

Blacks Created Great Communities

There is absolutely nothing that cannot be achieved in unity.

In the Christian faith, the bible records that when the children of the world gathered to build a tower that would reach into the heavens, God immediately scattered them because He saw that their resolve would bring what they desired to pass.

The same resolve can be found in Black people all across the world, as we are known for helping each other to do great things. Not too long ago and still currently, Black people are creating their own successful cities in America and across the globe.

Let us take for example the Greenwood neighborhood created in Tulsa, Oklahoma which became a successful economic district that it was being referred to as the 'Black Wall Street".

Let us shift attention to the other part of the globe; Africa, where we will take the example of Rwanda.

Sadly, the white man's propaganda is usually geared at making everyone believe that everything that comes out of Africa is death, famine, starvation and horrors.

The images on the media broadcasts usually picture the continent as one that is pitch dark with chaos and this makes some brainwashed Black people to disassociate themselves from this great continent.

In the case of Rwanda, the country experienced genocide in 1994 and since then, they established a truth and reconciliation board that ensured that the victims of the genocide were recompensed. Due to the fact that the genocide wrecked their country, just like Adolf Hitler's genocide wrecked Germany, Rwandans took upon themselves the task of nation-building. Brick by Brick, government policy-by-policy and speech-by-speech, they slowly rebuilt their society and currently have one of the best countries in Africa now.

Let us shift our focus back to the Black Wall Street that was created in Greenwood, Tulsa.

Black people have always been individuals who are filled with insight and the desire to create something great out of the seaming insurmountable chaos that are before them.

Nelson Mandela did this by fighting against the Apartheid system in South Africa, Malcolm X and Rev King did this by fighting the oppressive system that kept Black people in the shadows while Barack Obama fought against the exclusive system that kept Blacks in the shadow of power. We have done it and we still continue to do it.

In the case of the Black Wall Street, O.W. Gurley in 1906 was a well-to-do African America who was a native of Arkansas. Gurley made the move to Tulsa where he bought more than 40 acres of land that he only sold to Black people. He was also one of the great figures of our history because he provided his land as a source of protection for Black people who were running away from the oppressive Southern state of Mississippi.

Money stayed within

The events that followed showed that Black people are capable of doing anything when they unite.

By ensuring that it was only Black people who were able to buy lands in this area, many Black families moved in and began to build their businesses in a thriving area where they would not experience any sort of discrimination or threat to life.

Another consequence of creating this kind of settlement was that money began to circulate and stayed within the Black community as against other places where the money was passed down from the White man.

There is no mistaking the fact that the white man did everything he could to break down this community by targeting their morale and businesses at some points but the Black residents were resolute. A study that was conducted by stbayview.com showed that the dollar circulated 36 to 100 times and one brilliant thing that happened was that more than six African American families owned their personal planes at a time when the entire state of Oklahoma had only 2 airports.

This statistic may seem a bit normal to you because we are in the age of private jets but I am talking about the early 1900s. A time when the odds were grossly stacked against the Black man and a period where the White community were still openly using racism to beat down the Black man's pride. According to surveys, it was recorded that the average income for a Black family was very high and this meant that the standard of living for Black people was high

Burned during Race Riots

From the onset of this book, I told you that the white man is insanely jealous of you and he is not happy that you are always at the top in whatever thing you find yourself. I showed you my personal example at age 11 of how white children are also angry at the fact that you are superior to them.

Well, it seems that the local white neighbors in Tulsa began to take sips out of the hate poison and got jealous of the successes of their Black neighbors. Hatred is one of the worst negative vices because it blinds the eyes of the hater to his own deficiencies while making him boil with rage at the success story of other people.

The White community that was led by the Ku Klux Klan began a campaign that was aimed at denying the Black people the necessary things that they needed. When they realized that the Black people were not going to be deterred and would continue to build better houses and ride nicer cars, the Whites organized a riot that lasted over the course of 16 hours.

As the riot raged on, the whites raced into Black homes and torched them and when the entire community was burnt down, more than 800 people were hospitalized and a greater number close to ten thousand people became homeless. The resulting consequence of the fire to the economic life of the community was that more than 600 successful Black businesses were lost which included about twenty-one dinners, thirty grocery shops, 2 movie theatres and a black-owned hospital.

Can you imagine with within the space of some years of settling down, Tulsa Black families had built these unique businesses that even benefitted most of the White settlers in the area. However, the nature of hatred is that it would drive a person to destroy the place he is benefitting from just to spite the person he hates.

It is logically for us to think that the White community would have been encouraged to build their own successful businesses and ask for help from the Black communities but the white people there were just simply jealous of the nicer things of life which the Black community were enjoying.

The Rebuilding

As a result of their homes burnt to the ground and the halt of their businesses, the Black community at Tulsa was distraught for a while but they bounced back in full force.

The nature of the Black people is that we can never be boxed into a corner for long because we would always find a way to rise. We all possess the same blood as Muhammad Ali and this means that we will continue to rise and sting like a bee through our successes. Though the white man may stand in the opposite side of the ring and pay the referee to make the fight go his way, we always continue to emerge victorious because we are born to be victorious.

The Black residents of the community successfully rebuilt the vibrant Tulsa community and it continued to thrive until the period of 1950 and 1960 when desegregation set in and Black people had the opportunity to move to other places with the aim of recreating the success of the Black Wall Street.

No amount of propaganda can wash away the memory of the Black Wall Street from the history books because it stands as one of the proudest moments when Black people came together, under great distress, and established their own community which caused so much hate ripples with many white people. The memory of Black Wall Street shows that Black people are not destined to remain in low-income housing or ghettos for life. We are not meant to be clumped together in the 'other side' of town and we are not certainly meant to be denied most basic needs.

Unfortunately in some occasions, some Brainwashed Black politicians have bought this propaganda that is peddled by the White man and they feel that these low-income houses are the best option for Black people.

I urge you to ensure that every Black politician brushes up his or her history texts in order to know about the Black Wall Street. When they do that, they would be instantaneously challenged to dream bigger in terms of building projects which are being proposed for the Black community while rejecting the propaganda of the white man.

Another thing that we can learn from this Black Wall Street memory is that Black people should try to build their communities. Building your community would mean that you are proactive towards the creation of social amenities for your local community and it also means that you have the general welfare of Black people in your mind when making your decisions.

When Rosa Parks refused to stand up in that Montgomery Bus, she had the general welfare of the Black people in mind as she felt it was high time that African Americans should be treated like first-class citizens in their own country.

At a time when Malcolm X was threatened by the white superiority and the authorities with their dogs, hoses and legal systems, he never backed down in his ideology as he truly believed that the Black man must be freed of every political, social and most especially mental shackles.

It has been more than 40 years that Malcolm X has left the shores of the earth but some Black people remain in that mental shackle. Reading this book frees you from such mental shackles and it then becomes important that you become an agent of light that brings the illuminating light of Enlightenment to everyone in your community.

Ensure that you organize community events wherein the History of the Black man is taught with pride. Get the opinions of other members of the community about the best way which your community can match the successes of the Black Wall Street and also enlist the services of Black economists who can come up with concrete economic plans for your community.

Make sure that everyone in the community is carried along in this community building exercise especially your kids who would be the ones to carry the torch once you have left. Get your kids to understand the need to apply the educational knowledge they have acquired from Ivy League schools in their community so that they do not build other white businesses while Black communities continue to pine away.

Try and make the young ones understand the need for patience in building because the task of building your community would be arduous while they would encounter discouragement from the whites who usually take up interest in any Black emerging community.

Be Inspired By Your History

History is a tool that can be used to achieve various ends. Civil rights activists like Rev. Martin Luther King, Malcolm X and Nelson Mandela made references to the glorious history of Black people to spur the people towards demanding for change from their oppressors. In both instances given, the use of history worked like magic because the German people, as at the time, walked with dignity and treated Jews like animals while Black people began to walk with dignity and requested for a radical upgrade in status.

Black people should know that their history is not summed up by images of people being dragged across great mountains to the coast and then taken across the Atlantic to the 'New World'.

Those images constitute just a small fraction of your entire history so why should you be so much obsessed with them? There are greater images that have not made their way into the big screen motion pictures. Historical accounts of Glorious African Kings and Queens like Queen Amina of Zaria who led her people to engage in great expeditions where they defeated numerous lands and ended up building walled cities that even rivaled that of the Romans.

I know you would not have heard of these great periods of Black History because your History teachers are so obsessed with showing you a video of Roots and then going on to tell you some nonsense about you having a traumatic history.

No.

Roots and other videos like it do not capture the true glories of the Black Race. It does not capture the fact that Black people are the first on earth neither does it capture the fact that we were the ones that built the first human society in order to protect ourselves against the wild and also pooled our resources together to guarantee safety.

The books written by White historians will tell you that civilization came with the whites but that has always been a blatant lie that you ought to resist.

Now let us examine some of our living edifices that showcase the greatness of the Black people.

Oprah Winfrey

Oprah has become what can be tagged a religion due to the fact that her influence has cut across every field within America.

Her path to becoming the most beloved talk-show host, book club president, actress, magazine owner among other listless achievements that still continue to flood in, has not been one that has been paved with rose petals.

Rather, she is the typical personification of a strong Black woman who stared the monster called 'challenge' in its face and defeated it at its own chessboard.

Do you think she has not faced the same challenges that you have faced? The truth is that she has faced the challenge of overcoming the propaganda set in motion by the White man that is aimed at suppressing any good thing from Black people.

Many doors would have been shut in her face and she would have been 'politely' told to shut down most of the revolutionary ideas that she had because they were not expected to reside in the head of a Black person.

Oprah at the moment stands tall as a true heroine who inspires every Black person. When your daughter feels that she is never going to be great in life because her white friends think so, show her a portrait of Oprah and proudly tell her that Oprah is a worthy role model to follow.

When kids in your neighborhood make offhanded statements that whites will always bring down Blacks, point them in Oprah's way and tell them of a woman who is not only a Billionaire but one that is creating so much value that she is being sought after across the globe.

Oprah has become a brand. A 'made of black' brand that showcases one of the precious gems among Black people.

Kenneth Frazier

He was the first African-American Chief Executive Officer of Merck & Co., Inc that is a pharmaceutical company. His story is one of pure inspiration as he rose to the top of the echelon of his field and began to dominate.

One unique thing about him is that as a pro-bono Lawyer, he was able to don the superman cape and save a wrongly accused Alabama man from death row.

He fought against the self-limiting factors of his mind when he was still selling newts and tadpoles at Penn state. He believed in the greatness of his mind and was not afraid to dare despite the challenges that stood in his way to the top.

Now the CEO of one of the largest company in the globe, he is a source of inspiration that every Black person draws from. Many

Black charities have also benefited from Kenneth Frazier that exemplifies the reality that Black people are not the type of people that forget their people when they reach a position of influence.

We have always been a closely knit community that is driven by passion for excellence and that is why you should endeavor to always uphold this standard of supporting Black people in any way you can.

Ursula Burns

"It is a man's world."

This quip remains one that is true at all times as women have often played second fiddle throughout the course of history.

Even though the feminist movement is currently seeking to right the wrong by maintaining that both sexes are equal and are entitled to equal rights, it is still very difficult for women to rise to the top of any field.

Women of African American descent have had it in a tougher way than white women however as they have two factors working against them.

First, the White system is working to restrict them from ever becoming successful and then the male patriarchy sometimes finds it difficult to allow a woman break through to the top.

This is the major reason why the story of Ursula Burns remains an incredible source of inspiration as she rose to the top of her field by becoming the CEO of Xerox and was ranked the 14th most powerful woman in the world as at 2009.

You cannot begin to imagine the hurdles that Ursula had to scale through as she rose among the ranks in her workplace. Many people would have sworn never to work under a Black woman and then gone ahead to work against her progress but she toughened her skin in order to stay afloat.

It is easy to see here that the process of reaching the top entails you to toughen up your hide, as it will be pierced with many darts of hatred and disappointments. Every Black person should not only be inspired to succeed when reading about Ursula Burns but should be inspired to face challenges as they are the building blocks that will take them to the top.

Ursula's educational pedigree is one that serves to put the white man's propaganda to shame as she went to top colleges in the country where she got high grades before beginning her career as a summer intern with Xerox in 1980.

Another salient lesson that you should immediately point out for your benefit and the benefit of your kids is that it took her almost 29 years to reach the top yet she stayed. The lesson inscribed within is that the process of building sustainable success takes a while. It is usually a long process because you will need to internalize every lesson and if you stay committed to the process, you would reach the top and possess the tools that will make you stay at the top for long.

Remember the Black Wall Street example that was given earlier? They had the resources to build and reach the top but their safety was out of their hands and that was why it was easy for the jealous white community to organize the riot that brought the burning down of the community.

We are in the 21st century and to some extent, what you build can be protected and you can also learn better ways to insulate your success against failure.

Madame C.J Walker.

Madame Walker is another heroine character in the Black people's book of inspiration. She was also known as Sarah Breedlove and she is recorded as the first woman of African-American origin to become a millionaire from the creation of a workable salve.

Her story will continue to resound in our memories even though there are no motion films dedicated to her. Her legacy still remains as she has inspired Black people to always make something great out of every disappointing situation.

In her case, Madame Walker began to experience hair loss at an early age and she did not sit back to mope about her lost hair.

In most cases, many people who encounter physical challenges of any nature choose to blame it on God and continue with the belief that they are incapacitated from being able to address the defect. Madame Walker showed herself to be a visionary who thinks outside the box by experimenting with home products until she got the final solution that worked for her.

Black people should learn that even though the odds seem to be stacked against us, we are to think outside the box and become visionaries who would become sources of inspiration for our descendants in the future. Even after Madame Walker got the formula that solved her challenge, she was not selfish with it as the White media wants us to believe about Black people.

Rather, she decided to share this innovation with the Black community and since it was an innovation that brought value, she was naturally paid for it. Her story is also inspiring to little Black girls because their self-esteem would be boosted since they can identify with a Black woman who performed a feat which no one thought would be possible; she became a millionaire.

Adopting the Mindset of Winners

Now that you have been exposed to the tools that the White man uses to brainwash Black people, it is pertinent to come up with your own winning formula that would counteract those tools while you proceed on your way to the top. Your mindset is the tool that I am going to sharpen in this chapter with particular emphasis on how you can totally renew its contents in a way that it would work for you and not against you.

A vital key point that you should retain is this;

"You BECOME what you PRACTICE"

Anything you fixate your attention upon over the course of time begins to radiate on you.

If you are so much fixated on soccer till the extent that you live and breathe statistics and recognize every play within the book as well as the individuals who made the spot popular, the chances that you will become excellent at soccer are very high.

The same thing happens when you begin to fix your mind on the practice of something. Let us take the case of Oprah Winfrey who is a very celebrated talk show host.

In order to become a talk show host who doles out advice to millions at every coverage, you must engage in series of set forward activities that must be routinely practiced. One of such activities is reading because, in order to give, you must have something inside you.

Reading opens the mind to limitless possibilities as it exposes you to the minds of other people and this makes you have an added advantage.

In order to become a successful talk show host as well, Oprah must have mastered the art of asking questions that would trigger the necessary emotions that she is after. While you may think that asking questions is easy, you would be shocked to realize that the process of asking the right questions that would not sound stupid is very difficult.

Also, the person who is to become a Talk show host will be someone who has practiced staying in front of a crowd for so long that they would feel no stage jitters at all. If you think it is easy to stand before a crowd of three hundred and have cameras focused on you, you will realize that it is one of the most difficult things because there is something that will keep informing you that your entire reputation is on the line since you are being watched by millions.

Muhammad Ali

Muhammad Ali is another Black person who typifies what the above advice is.

Ali did not jump into the ring on the first day and knock out his opponents. He had to spend many hours jogging in the streets in order to build up his stamina, stay in the boxing gym for many hours at the punching bag in order to build up his strength as well as speed.

All these activities were not done in a haphazard manner. Rather, himself and his team meticulously set training's in order and he faithfully followed through because he could not afford to miss any bit.

The process of becoming successful is preceded by a period of crazy practice. A period where you channel all your vitality in the practice till you are fully spent in terms of emotion and mentally.

Your practice time is the time when you hang a signpost that says "no disturbance". That signpost is meant to be read by everyone around you and not excluding family because in order to provide value to them, you must be separated!

The question I want to ask you as a Black Achiever is, "Where is your practice ring?" Your practice ring is the arena where you sit and learn under various coaches that include patience, books and mentors.

You get to shut up and listen as these coaches drum life's lessons into your hearing in a bid to sharpen you for the challenges.

The practice ring is also the place where you get to fight numerous undercard fighters who would usually end up knocking you out at the first try. Be rest assured, you will come back stronger after standing up.

You will also face the fighter called 'propaganda' who will knock you down many times before you will get ahold of his tactics and then go on towards defeating him.

Another undercard fighter that will deal with you in the practice area is loneliness. It is often said that the road to the top is lonely and this is the reason why you will have to fight him. You will be lonely at most points because most people will never understand your desire to be better at what you are doing. Even though they understand, most of them will not recognize the need to isolate yourself more in the practice area and that is why you will be lonely.

Nevertheless, since you have chosen to aim higher, your practice level will occur more frequently because it is not enough to reach the top. Floyd Mayweather retired as a boxing champion not because the caliber of fighters that faced him were small, but because he kept on practicing like his life depended on the fight.

His swift maneuvers, quick heavy punches and victories were sole products of his doggedness at the boxing ring.

Winners vs. Losers

Who can you define as a winner and how can you distinguish such a person from a loser?

The reason why this is important is that the duos are often members of the same social clubs attend the same dinners often and also have the same types of personalities. You get to see that winners and losers may be outgoing or withdrawn in their persona and that is the reason why it is really difficult to distinguish one from the other.

However, let me quickly tell you three attributes that you can use to distinguish a winner from a loser.

- Attitudes

- Behavioral patterns

- The results they achieve

The duo are not the same when they are contrasted with these three characteristics and it is noteworthy to state that a winner can become a loser if he or she begins to adopt the same type of attitudes, behavioral patterns and results of the loser and vice versa.

Attitude

Attitude is everything because success and failure begins as an attitude. When a little child is born, there is a theory that states that the little child is a tabula rasa that means that the child is a blank slate.

Day after day, the child begins to learn things from the environment: things like the smell of her mother's perfume, or the sound of his father's voice. The child begins to particularly learn the language and also how the parents play.

This is often the reason why some children become addicted to trying to act like their parents in order to please them sometimes and you see some other children gravitating towards the kind of careers that their parents lead.

The lesson I want you to draw from this place is that in most cases, attitudes are learnt from our parents and our environment. The consequence of this is that many Black parents need to start being conscious of the way they act around their children especially at an age when those children are learning everything you do and are imitating you. This is the age you can easily condition that child to become an achiever.

Let us examine some attitudes that you can begin to exercise in order to inculcate that winning mentality within yourself and in your child;

1. Read books-

Listen well, there is no other antidote that can help you solve the problem of propaganda than reading, a lot!

There is a widely depressing statistic that claim that Black people do not like to read and particular films try to showcase Black people as those who are afraid of reading but this is not true.

Nevertheless, if you want to become an achiever, you must learn the art of reading and enjoying what you read. Reading does not need to be a boring time wherein you force yourself to read something you don't want to.

Rather, a productive reading time is one that you spend time reading what will drive you to the top of your career.

For example, let us say you are a low time screenwriter who wants to make it big and write blockbuster movies like Hidden Figures etc. You will have to read novels extensively in order to stimulate your creative mind.

You would also need to read the works of other screenwriters whose advice would help you avoid the mistakes that limited them. As a budding screenwriter as well, you would have to read books that teach you how to pitch your screenplays to the best production companies and the best way to handle rejections since they will come.

Let us examine another scenario. Let us say you are a nurse who wants to guarantee financial freedom for yourself. I believe that you should begin to read works that talk on the best nurse practices in the entire globe.

You can advance your interest towards books that teach on the power of words and how to encourage patients because this would set you apart in your craft.

Also, it is important that you begin to read books that talk on the latest technological advancements in the field of nursing so that you can begin to think of an idea technology that would aid patients in your field.

That idea creation stage would be fueled when you read more books to know if it has been done before and from books, you can know the process of getting your invention ready which range from the idea formation to getting it approved by the FDA and then getting it patented after you.

Cultivate the habit of reading to your little ones as they grow because you will soon inculcate that same habit within them and if you are thinking that it would be too difficult to read hard copy books, you can get audiobooks. However, ensure that you also read with hard copy books at times because it psychologically disassociates you from distractions and most times discourages people from trying to disturb you.

2. Speaking Positively:

What has speaking positively got to do with anything?

Well, studies have shown that even animals and plants react differently to positive and negative words.

Have you ever screamed at your dog or your cat in a bid to get it to do something? You would notice that their happy moods are immediately shut down and they would walk sulkily to perform the action you want.

However, when you speak to them in a loving way, you are going to get the desired result of happiness because the dog would wag its tail cheerfully and even offer playful barks to show her love for you.

Now let us go to the study of plants.

A group of scientists gathered themselves with the aim of discovering if plants reacted to sounds differently or were indifferent to it.

For this study, they gathered a group of plants and put them in two different rooms. In a period of the first two weeks, they took note of the plants progress within the two weeks, as they did not play any sound in the room. The result was that the plants in both rooms grew at the same pace.

After this first stage, the scientists took out the plants and put in another set of plants in the two rooms. Then in room A, they always made sure that they played calm sounds which were sure background sounds for positive messages while in room B, they blasted a rage-filled music that is mostly used to propagate messages like hate and negativity.

After a week, the scientists came to look at the project and the results were mind-blowing. In Room A where the calm sounds played, the plants experienced what could be tagged as 'accelerated growth' as they were luxuriant and blossoming more than the plants of the previous set. Then, when the scientists went to the other room that contained the other plants that were exposed to rage sounds, they discovered that most of the plants had withered and died. The few plants that were still alive showed signs of increasing deterioration.

In order to confirm if their findings were truly concrete, the scientists switched music and the rage music was being played in room A while the calm, reassuring music was being played in the room of the dying plants. Within the space of a week as well, the scientists confirmed their finding as they discovered that the once blooming plants from room A began to experience signs of deterioration while the dying plants from room B experienced a slow and steady growth with their leaves becoming green once more.

Have you ever seen an elderly man bent over his garden and singing good songs as he tends to his plants? It is because he understands the power of positive music and in a conscious way; the plants accustom themselves to the voice of the owner and feel reassured.

The reason why you have to speak reassuring positive words to yourself and around your children is that they will grow up with the kind of words that they are accustomed to. If you are the type of person that loves to tell yourself that you are incapable of engaging in a task because you are a Black person or because you are a woman, you will soon get to realize that your child will not ever see anything good about himself or herself because she/is Black as well.

This is part of the problem of the entire country as well because there is a disheartening statistics that show that many marriages collapse within their first three years. When you tend to ask what the reason for the collapse was, most times you discover that one of the spouses picked up a learned habit of quitting early from the parents and when they hit a little patch in their wedding, they decide to immediately quit because there is no toughness within them.

Whenever you are with your children, ensure you speak in a positive way so that they inculcate the right attitude.

3. Value chase

By chasing after value, I mean that you should always esteem value creation over profit in everything you do as it will be one of the most vital lessons that you will pass down to your child.

These days, many people seek the quick fame, the large bucks without taking time to discover the type of values they can give away.

Black people have been known to be individuals who place premium on the value of brotherhood and this is a tradition that must continue to be upheld.

I believe that I should state at this point that the pursuit of success might not always yield fat bank accounts; luxury yacht cruises to the Bahamas or weekly trips with your kids to Disneyland.

While all these will be nice, you should understand that being successful entails creating something that would be a source of joy for people in the long run.

Take Malcolm X for example. Our brother was not one that owned private jets or went on cruise boating trips around the world but he still proved to be a success while he lived and is still being celebrated in his death.

Why? The reason he was successful was because he stood up for the rights of Black people and advocated that we must forcefully collect our freedom if the white superiority is not ready to give it peacefully.

Nelson Mandela who is affectionately known as Madiba and the father of the nation of South Africa was not a billionaire while he lived. Rather, he was someone that bravely withstood the Apartheid authorities and spent 27 years in prison still fighting for what he believed in.

You can teach your kids this truth by always chasing after value yourself.

What inventions are you planning and how will that invention be of benefit to mankind?

What kind of business am I going to engage in and how will it be of personal good to the Black community that I am a resident in?

What am I going to study in school and how can it be of importance to Black people in general?

You should be able to answer these questions at every time because losers can be people who are rich but do not provide any form of value to anyone.

A Black person who is a millionaire by cheating other Black people and not even giving back to the community is a sore loser because the person is only holding on to wealth that ought to be beneficial to every other person.

What will be the purpose of living life in a way that is extremely selfish and being forgotten in death because you did not provide anything for the black community when you are alive?

Black icons today like LeBron James, Magic Johnson and others are epitomes of success because they have also helped other people grow and did not forget their roots when they became famous. Simply put, they broke the white propaganda that says that black people are like crabs in a barrel who are only good at dragging themselves down

Behavioral Patterns of Winners

This is another characteristic that differentiates winners from losers.

The first behavioral pattern that you will easily notice with winners is that they place *premium on alliances.*

Let me quickly tell a quick history of European nations in order to show you the essence of building alliances.

1870-1871 was a pivotal year in Europe as it witnessed the outbreak of a war between France and Prussia. Prussia was the new name that was given to the Germanic states that had united together with Otto Von Bismarck as their chancellor. When the war broke out, the newly emerged Prussian state defeated France in a decisive way and took over Alsace Lorraine that was a very fertile region.

Immediately after the defeat, the German chancellor begin to engage in a series of visits to countries like Britain, Austria and Russia and the main aim of visiting these countries was to sign military alliances with them in order to starve France of any form of Friendship.

The military alliance was needed for Prussia because it meant that France would not think of attacking her again since the alliance stated that the signatory countries would fight for each other when attacked. Through the years up till 1910, Germany kept up these alliances until a very immature man stepped to the throne and then began to think he could wage war on his own without any alliance.

All this while, France had been waiting on the wings and immediately, she moved in and began to sign alliances with Britain and Russia who Germany abandoned. The World War I started in 1914 and it was Germany against the other countries that ended with a devastating German defeat in 1918.

The lesson was learned; *alliances are key.*

Within the Black entertainment culture, you can see how alliances have helped individual artists who were little known, transform into big household Artists who are still renowned today. Think of the dynamic alliance that was forged between Eminem and Dr. Dre and the platinum awards they won together as a team.

Think of the Jackson Brothers and how their initial alliance was able to launch Michael Jackson into the spotlight.

You can also think of the Destiny Child that featured Beyoncé Kelly Rowland and Michelle Williams and how it proved to be a launch pad that launched Beyoncé into becoming the global star she is now.

Let us not forget the 'We are the world' collaborative songs that have been produced to raise awareness for important life-threatening events in the world like the Haitian humanitarian crisis.

In all these instances, you get to see that they recognized that building alliances in not just a necessity but a rule for those who wish to become winners.

Take a look at losers.

They are always in a solitary state because they think that their genius is simply enough to guarantee them front row seats in the hall of fame. The problem is that even though they are brilliant, they would not be able to take off and fly because there would be no one around them to help them launch forward.

At the times when they would be mentally down and in need of allies to cheer them up, they would recognize that there is nobody and this can make them slip into depression.

Let me show you how a classic case of alliances can make our communities better.

Imagine a building complex filled with numerous businesses. Even though the businesses within the complex experience some level of growth, they would experience a greater level of growth if they simply put their businesses together with one shop.

How does this work, you ask?

If you are the owner of a Dentist establishment and you share a floor with a spa business along with a flight ticketing company, you can all decide to move in together and any client who comes in for teeth checkup may decide to immediately move to the spa section after the dentist session because they are both in the same office. The same thing can apply to a client who came to book flight tickets and in turn goes in for a quick dental checkup.

The benefit of this alliance is that there would be lesser cost spent on rent, design while you are definitely going to get more customer base.

However, if you plan on engaging in this kind of business alliance, you should look to build alliances with another Black entrepreneur whose business is complementary to your own.

What this means is that when your client immediately finishes a session with you, the other business that you share the same office with should be one that should immediately interest them. You cannot place a dentist shop and an ice cream shop in the same office because they would not be complimentary at all.

Winners build quality alliances because they realize that such alliances will easily propel them to the top of their fields.

Winners get results

Take note of this line of reasoning because it applies to both winners and losers alike;

Your attitude will drive your behavior and your behavior automatically drives your success rate

No winner is renown for having a history of past failures with no single success. This is one thing that is easily noticeable when it concerns winners because a history of near misses does not qualify for success.

Do not think that your well-documented history of nearly winning the crown will eventually get your name etched in the book of winners because it does not work that way.

Some people choose to remain where they are and the White superiority will want you to think that it is okay for Black people to play the second role to the white man. This is a line of thinking which you must reject in a fervent manner. If others choose to remain stagnant and choose to smile in second position, you should not because we are kings and Queens.

Even from the religious perspective, it is recorded that our creator gave us the strict injunction to be fruitful, multiply and DOMINATE!

Winners dominate by producing concrete results. At a point in the life of Barack Obama when he saw that he was not achieving the results he needed, he switched tactics and got the exact thing he chased after.

Stevie Wonder, Ray Charles, James Brown and other Black singers who remain some of the greatest musicians ever, understood that winners always get results and that is why they were not relenting in churning out musical records consistently.

At the point when they felt that their brand of music was becoming repetitive, they ensured that they switched their style up and turned up the notch of their rehearsals. They remained dogged and kept on pushing until the thing they desired became their reality.

Winners are never afraid of change

At this point, you should have taken note that most of the Black icons which this book has mentioned shared one thing in common which was the ability to stop doing something at a time and begin another.

The thing about change is that most people recognize its need but few actually make the effort to try. The reason why change is difficult is that you have become so accustomed to one pattern of getting things done that even if it stops working, you may continue to remain obstinate in your zeal to make it work and you end up wasting quality time.

The human brain is a mechanism that works with ease when it engages itself in performing a series of programmed activities. For example, for Black people who have been programmed to think that their history started with slave trade, their brain conditions them to depend on the white man and it also teaches them to always recognize anything belonging to the white man as superior and associates anything Black with 'inferior'.

Breaking free of such mentality is possible but it will be a difficult process for the brains of such Black people.

The brains of winners are quite different from that of losers because it has become accustomed to the concept of change. Winners are never afraid of cutting loose with some investments when they recognize its inability to yield fruits in the future.

In apparent opposition, Losers, even though seeing that a business is not viable, choose to stick to saving it because they are afraid of starting all over again with newer resources. In that way, such losers become captains who try to save a sinking ship that has already been flooded with water.

The idea that you should continue a business because you have invested so much in it, should not cross your mind especially in the occasion that the business has lost its viability. It is just like Apple trying to hold on to selling a computer that has a very slow operating system when Microsoft launches a superfast computer.

This line of thinking is not exclusive to you because most people tend to jump on the bandwagon of sticking to what is popular without being the visionary that would create something new.

You should not be afraid to dump what is new in search for what you think will be the future. That is the way inventions are made.

Winners are always tinkering with new stuff.

Winning music producers are always experimenting with newer beats.

Winning Black teachers are always experimenting newer techniques that would make their classes more engaging.

Winning couples are always willing to improve every aspect of their relationship including tinkering with acts you would not believe if you heard.

Successful athletes such as Usain Bolt are always thinking of better diets that can make them achieve optimal levels of success.

Winning book authors are always tinkering with newer concepts which can help them break into newer markets.

Winning actors and actresses like Denzel Washington, Gabriella Union, Taraji P. Henson among others are always ready to break out from the comfortable roles they are accustomed to in order to star in roles that they are not comfortable with. Even though they may fail in getting the accolades at the release of such movies, movie fans generally end up showering them with accolades since the actors and actresses chose to leave the comfortable roles they have perfected.

This vital fact of life will also be beneficial to your kids as they would acquire a learned behavior of dynamic change. However, there are occasions when you would only need to exhibit some patience for the process you initiated to settle and yield the needed result.

Your Magnificent Mind.

Let's assume for a minute that your mind is a really powerful computer. It has its own software that helps you organize your thinking and behavior. If you are exhibiting a behavior pattern that you want to change, it's just a matter of changing your programming. This process is called 'Mental Conditioning'.

The problem is that you are not in control of your initial programming. You are born with a blank disk in your hard drive; so to speak. So where does your initial programming come from? Well, the simple answer is that it is a product of your parents. But this is not entirely true because, then you have to ask yourself..."where did my parents programming come from?"

Herein lies the problem for you in particular, and for Black people in general.

Your basic programming, which is the foundation of everything you build your life upon, was given to you indirectly by slave owners. I know that is hard to believe because slavery happened so long ago but it is the truth. The slave owners programmed the first slaves in this country to believe that they were inferior. They were programmed to believe that black skin is bad: that blacks are lazy, untrustworthy, sex addicted and uneducated buffoons. These are the same things you and I are told to believe about Black people to this day. It is passed down from generation to generation and reinforced every time you see a movie or watch television.

This poison does not only make white people believe that Black people are inferior but it also causes you to think Black people are inferior sometimes which is even more destructive for you since you are a Black person. This way of thinking is called 'self-hatred'. I have met thousands of Black people from all over the world and we all practice self-hatred at some point in our lives. You have exhibited if you have ever thought in terms of light skin versus dark skin, or told someone they have good hair versus the nappy hair you think is inferior. The list goes on and on and this is so normal in our culture that we don't even realize we are doing it.

You have been basically programmed to despise yourself. How crazy does that sound? And if that is not crazy enough, white people have taught the entire world that is perfectly normal to despise Black People too.

Racism and its negative physiological effects affect every Black person. For example: Oprah Winfrey, one of America's best-loved television personalities, one of the world's richest women and top of the Forbes' list of 100 most powerful celebrities is not immune from racism.

The US talk show host, said at a time that she was the victim of racism during a visit to Switzerland where she was attending Tina Turner's wedding.

Winfrey said a shop assistant refused to serve her in a high-end Zurich handbag shop. The foolish assistant had said that the bags on offer were "too expensive" for Oprah.

The TV star said she left the shop without contesting the shop assistants' behavior and that episode contributed to her experience on a debate about the continued existence of racism on a US television show.

Winfrey told Entertainment Tonight: "I was in Zurich the other day, in a store whose name I will not mention. I didn't have my eyelashes on, but I was in full Oprah Winfrey gear. I had my little Donna Karan skirt and my little sandals. But obviously, The Oprah Winfrey Show is not shown in Zurich."

"I go into a store and I say to the woman, 'Excuse me, may I see the bag right above your head?' and she says to me, 'No. It's too expensive.'"

When Winfrey insisted she did want to see the bag, the shop assistant allegedly replied: "No, no you don't want to see that one, you want to see this one because that one will cost too much. You will not be able to afford that."

Winfrey, who is a billionaire, continued: "There's two different ways to handle it. I could've had the whole blow-up thing" And when asked if racism still exists, she replied..."of course it does."

Why then does this matter to you? It matters because winning is hard. Going for your life goals is the hardest thing you will ever do. You will be scared. You will doubt yourself you will face extraordinary setbacks along the way. In order to overcome the challenges that stand in your way, you cannot subconsciously believe that you are inferior. And you can't let other people treat you like you are inferior. You have to stand up for yourself. Because if you subconsciously believe this about yourself and allow people to treat you in a negative way, you have virtually no chance of achieving your goals.

Now, I know what you are saying to yourself..."I would never think I am inferior." And I agree with you. You would never think this on a conscious level. But on a subconscious level, you can think this because it is part of the negative propaganda that is bombarding your mind. My goal is to help you to remove this destructive programming from your unconscious mind. And once you have read this book you will have the tools needed to destroy this self-hatred program that is running in the recesses of your mind.

Now let's explore the difference between your conscious mind and your unconscious mind.

Your Conscious Mind

Everything about our existence is based on how we make sense of them. Our activities, convictions, belief systems, speech and every other thing are really framed by our conscious and unconscious mind.

The conscious mind is one that you actively make use of throughout your life in shaping your activities, belief systems. When you wake in the morning, you make conscious effort to get out of bed and engage in your daily traditions that may include meditation and prayer, checking up with your family, reading an excerpt from a book or writing down the things that are needful.

Being a person who is in pursuit of success, you must begin to harness the power of your conscious mind in setting plans in motion that would guarantee your success. You should not be found lollygagging about with your precious time because that is the greatest commodity that is available for everyone.

It is important that you train your conscious mind to recognize the essence of time management and never joke with it. When your conscious mind begins to beam its focus towards maximizing every second of the day, it would yield great fruits for you.

Most people do not really understand the principle of accountability. Perhaps when they hear the word, they switch off with the thinking that it is a word that belongs to the sphere of Economics and does not apply to them. For such people, life seems to always blaze past them and when they reach a certain age, they begin to be puzzled about the way time has passed by.

You need to train your mind to be accountable. How does this work?

The principle of Accountability simply states that you should take records of every action because you are responsible for everything.

This means that you should take record of how you spend every second of your day and account for everything you receive into your life. Do not attempt to live a carefree life where you do not take stock of your actions because the law of Karma exists and every action you take has a way of taking you closer to success or dragging you backwards.

Let us consider examples that will help to propel your pursuit of financial freedom.

Every great company pursues the particular principle of paying attention to details. Through the production process, they are careful to observe every stage as they recognize the fact that one little imperfection can ruin the product.

The same is applicable when such companies engage in market survey. In most occasions, the market survey is geared towards helping the company know how the clients feel concerning their products and how they will be receptive to new products. These companies do not fail to undertake this market survey and it forms one of the core attributes that make them remain at the top.

As regards with you, you must train your conscious mind to always utilize every opportunity that comes your way. It would also be needful to train it to pay attention to the minute details of your life so that you would not fall a victim of your own negligence.

Ensure that you apply your conscious mind to your speech with those you love so you don't end up making offhanded statements that may end up hurting their self-esteem.

Avoid things that dull your conscious mind

This is an important lesson that you should try to internalize because there is nothing more destructive than substances that are aimed at dulling your conscious mind.

Black people who have problems at their place of work and clashes with their spouses easily realize that drowning themselves in alcohol is just a temporary medicine that does not cure the problem.

Successful people are those that easily recognize their problems and move towards attending to it. They do not shy away from the problem because that would mean an extension of the time it would take to solve the problem.

As it has been proven times without number, most relationships tend to degenerate further when one of the partners decides to take the easy way out through alcohol.

Successful people are also wary of other kind of substances that change their perception of life. Narcotics of different kinds fall into this category of drugs that change the perception of the conscious mind. When consumed, such narcotics end up doing more harm than good as they lead the user down the hallway of addiction till they become empty shadows of their previous selves.

The white man's propaganda is aimed at making Black people rely more on drugs and alcohol so that we would not be able to focus on reaching the top of our various fields but they will continue to lose in their propaganda if Black people come together in complete rejection of these narcotics.

In your neighborhood, you should begin to lead a local campaign with the social message that the conscious mind is the most priceless tool that they should protect. When you engage in this sort of social campaign, you are creating a safe world where Black Kids would grow and pursue success with their conscious mind

Limitations of the Conscious mind

Irrespective of the numerous ways that the conscious mind helps us, it has its own limitation. The limitation of the conscious mind is that while you are able to detect imminent physical danger that may intend to harm, you are not able to detect psychological dangers that are more dreadful.

This book has mentioned one of the propaganda of the white man that is aimed at keeping you in a state of inaction. It has shown that most movies portray the entire 'Black experience' as one that is filled with slavery and torture but the aim is to weaken your self-confidence and make you have self-hatred for anything that is associated with Black.

Unfortunately for most Black people, they are unable to recognize this propaganda and the same trend happens to their children while they are incapable of putting an end to it.

A female professional who gave a powerful Ted talk pointed out another example, of how your conscious mind is limited. In the talk, she showcased the way in which the makers of Barbie were sometimes conditioning little girls to accept secondary roles within the society.

She stated that the Barbie brand released some Barbie dolls with manuals that portrayed Barbie as a helpless girl that needs the help of Boys to perform some roles in the society. She showed that the kind of message which that line of Barbie dolls sent was that girls are weaker than boys and that kind of social conditioning works towards the goal of making women remain in the shadows in the society.

Your conscious mind may at times not recognize the underlying message that is being passed across in most TV Commercials that always show Black women with long flowing hair as opposed to kinky short hair.

Your conscious mind may not easily pick out the attempt of the white system to keep Black people in a state of debt by offering credit cards to buy whatever we want.

Your conscious mind may not easily spot out the message being passed by most songs that material riches are the definition of true success and not the creation of value.

Even in most cases while you are watching the foreign news, your conscious mind will not show you that 90% of news items about Africa is always grim and depressing while the same statistic is not applicable to European countries.

You would not know that it is still part of the propaganda, as the white man does not want you to ever attribute anything good to Africa.

Even while watching the news, your conscious mind will not easily pick out the propaganda message that portrays Black youths as violent, drug-loving people who do not engage in any form of activity that brings value to humankind and the nation.

Your Unconscious Mind

The unconscious mind is the most powerful if there is a comparison undertaken with the conscious mind.

The reason why it remains more potent in scope is that it possesses the ability to process millions of sensory information every second and it is the storehouse where they reside till they are called into usage at spontaneous times that they are needed.

Have you ever wondered why at some point in your life, you can just easily remember a piece of information and then forget it immediately? This is a product of your unconscious mind in action and that is why you have to be mindful of the kind of information you expose yourself to so that you do not recall information that may be damaging to you at the moment you need it.

I want to take extra care to buttress on the need to consciously expose yourself to the right information because your subconscious mind is the bank that dispenses your creativity.

Poems remain sources of enigma to many people because they seem to emanate from a place of pure genius. The ability of Black poets like Maya Angelou and others to produce breathtaking moving poems that talk about experiences of love, war etc., is a product of the storehouse of their sub-conscious minds.

Throughout the course of their lives, they keep exposing themselves to abstract languages that their sub-conscious mind recalls for them when they begin to pen down their poetry.

Every Black achiever in the financial sphere understands this principle and that is why they consciously expose themselves to environments where their conscious mind learns principles of business and their unconscious mind documents everything about the environment including gestures, offhanded statements, pattern of arrangement etc.

When such Black achievers leave those environments and are in the process of achieving their goals, their sub-conscious mind helps them recall easy patterns to solve their challenges.

The unconscious mind provides a kind of 'Autopilot' role for your every action in the long run as it takes over the running of activities that have been pre-installed by your conscious mind in a while back.

Let us take an example of a plane or a helicopter.

It the case of both of them, they require the conscious mind of the pilot for them to take off the ground. When they both reach respectable heights, it is then that the flights can be put on autopilot mode wherein the plane or helicopter draws from its pre-installed flight manual in staying on-course to reach the destination it has been programmed to reach.

When you were a teenager trying to learn how to drive, you made a lot of mistakes that probably made a lot of pedestrians and other car owners to curse you right?

The fact is that this is the learning process where you get to learn how to quickly change your gears, or how to speed up- just in case the cops come around you.

The learning process you went through required that you used your conscious mind so that you can be able to stay focused. At the early stage of learning, you may not have made much use of your subconscious mind because there is not much to draw from though some people would have been able to draw the art of balance from their mind which their subconscious mind may have picked from previous activities like meditation etc.

After you pass through the stage of learning fully with your conscious mind, your subconscious mind begins to help you engage in the task of driving more often when your mind is troubled and you still need to drive. For example, in the occasion that you need to reach the hospital in full speed because of an emergency awaiting you, your conscious mind will engage itself in worry throughout the length of the journey while the subconscious mind will be the main driver that ferries you to the hospital.

Have you ever wondered how some drunken people get to drive to their homes without having the function of their conscious mind?

The answer is that they engage the use of their subconscious mind. After they are drunk and realize they have to get home, their subconscious mind begins to guide their limbs towards the car though they would stagger a lot. Their subconscious also drives for them and helps them recognize every marker that shows them how near or far away they are from their home.

Habits are always formed by the subconscious mind, as they are series of conscious actions and reactions that are recorded by the unconscious mind. That is how alcoholics become who they are. When they first experience loss of something or are faced with challenges that looked too big to handle, they sought for the location of the bar where they drank to dull their pain.

At that point, they are not yet alcoholics but are on the road towards reaching the destination. When the next time arrives with newer challenges and letdowns at work, such people still consciously took the option of drinking themselves to stupor in order to stop themselves from facing reality.

The subconscious mind is recording the triggers and the results at this point and when it happens at a third attempt, the subconscious mind takes over the reactions. This means that even though the person faces a new challenge and tries to consciously address the problem without drinking, his subconscious mind will flood him with an overwhelming urge to go towards the bar and pick up the bottle as a means to solving the problem.

Over time, this continues to happen and the way in which such chains of habit are broken is usually by acceptance of the fact that they are alcoholics.

What this means is that they accept the fact that their subconscious mind is the one that keeps pushing them towards the bottle and this means that they intend to begin an installation of a new set of actions that will replace that which the subconscious mind has programmed itself to do. If you have ever attended an Alcoholics Anonymous (AA) group session, you will notice that they always utter a string of positive words that would guide their future actions. Some may say;

I will not choose the bottle as an easy way out in the future

I can scale through this stage of alcoholism

The words of self-reassurance are continually uttered and while it does not seem to make any sense for the functioning alcoholic at the first set of meetings, it has profound effect of slowly breaking the hold of Alcohol on the subconscious mind.

Nevertheless, the members of the group have their own part to play in not indulging themselves to any drink whenever their nostrils are hit with the smell of their favorite drink or at the time when they encounter challenges at home and at work

Winners create their own habit

You are an achiever. As a matter of fact, you are a proud King and Queen that was created to rule and this is the reason why you will have to forge your own habits that will push you to the top.

You saw the way that alcoholics form their habits and overcome it? That is the way you will have to teach your subconscious mind to adopt the habits of a winner. Only that you will have to do this in reverse because you will have to break free of the habit of losers which you have already been used to.

What exactly is this habit of losers?

- It is the way they act nonchalantly towards the achieving of their goal.

- It is the way they easily give up in the process of success and then end of blaming other people for it instead of themselves.

- It is the way they try to stick to one course of action while expecting a different result.

- It is the way they easily spot out the defects of other people when they have the same defects as well.

- It is in the way they easily think that they can do it by themselves without needing any help.

- It is in the way they think that they do not need to provide value for humanity and that money would gravitate towards them suddenly.

- It is in the way that they ignore very important seasons of planting and ignore principles that are taught in books.

Losers have this mindset already preinstalled in their subconscious mind and if they are ever going to break away from such mentality, they would need to unlearn these habits.

Remember that we said that functional alcoholics often repeat a string of words that make no sense to them as at the point that they are being said? Every Black person will have to engage in the repetition of some words in order to break free of the hold of a loser's habit.

First, admit that you have been programmed by the white man to think of yourself as low and to always see good things coming from white people. Admit that you have been brainwashed into thinking that everything white is good while everything Black is bad. After you have accepted this, you have to speak positive self-assuring words such as;

The era of slavery does not determine who Black people are

Black people are the first to be created on this planet

I am meant to play the lead role and not the supporting cast of any race

I am a Queen who has the blood of great African queens in me

I am a king whose blood is flowing with the histories of great civilizations

I can do everything I want to do if I put my mind towards it

Nothing can stop me if I choose to move towards a direction because I am a tsunami that cannot be barricaded

These series of self-affirmative words have provided the background from which you can proceed to breaking the cycle of losing.

After you have said the words, you must now begin to engage in a fresh set of activities that would counter your subconscious mine.

Fresh actions that you will take include;

- Making it a point of duty to read everyday

- Making it a point of duty to always seek to better the Black community

- Making it a point of duty to account for every second of the day

- Making it a point of duty to always focus hard during the learning process of everything

- Making it a point of duty to endure personal insults at some periods of time in order to salvage a relationship

- Making it a point of duty to lead in every little place you find yourself

- Making it a point of duty to first become a loyal follower who takes note of the leader

- Making it a point of duty to approach people with the aim of building a strategic relationship

- Making it a point of duty to find a mentor who has excelled in your field and is willing to spare some time for you

- Making it a point of duty to always search for opportunities on a daily basis

- Making it a point of duty to impart what you have learnt to your immediate community without the aim of making profit.

- Making it a point of duty to start your day with positive affirmative words while shunning the despair brought on by the failure of yesterday

- Making it a point of duty to always look to the future with increased optimism and not fear

While engaging yourself in these fresh set of activities, I want you to know that your subconscious mind will flood you with overwhelming thoughts of abandoning them in order to stick to what it already knows before. Like an alcoholic fighting off the scent of his favorite beer, you must fight off the scent of actions like;

- Placing the blame of your failure on the fact that you are Black

- Placing the blame of your failure on the people that you are around

- Celebrating too early

- Sticking to the set of knowledge you know at all times.

In a gradual way, your subconscious mind will begin to unlearn the programmed activities of a loser and install the actions of a successful person that in turn transforms into habits.

Exercising Your Mind

The process of exercising your mind is one that entails the engagement of some forms of games and also writings.

In doing this, you can begin by finding a calm place and then let your mind roam. As your mind is roaming, keep a pen ready at hand and then let your mind flow with ideas from your subconscious mind. What this activity does is that it helps you determine the progress you are making with your subconscious mind while it helps to train it better because you can choose to actively block any incoming thought of negativity.

You should understand the gift of silence and embrace it. Silence is a period when you are insulated against the activities and ideas of people in order to listen to yours.

That is why you should cultivate a period of meditation on a daily basis so that you can be able to spare some silent moments for yourself. You are at your personal best at this period because your conscious mind is actively scrutinizing most of the content of your subconscious mind that gives you the opportunity to battle against every negative trace of self-limiting thought.

Check the schedule of every great person that you have ever heard of and you will notice that they do not joke with their moments of meditations.

Gospel preachers such as Bishop TD Jakes stress that it is at those moments that his spirit communes with God and the period when God reminds him of His love for Jakes.

For the Bishop, he is at his most creative best during such moments of silence because he is reminded of the things that God has dropped in his spirit in the bustle of the previous day.

Brother Malcolm X was another great Black person that understood the need for those silent periods of time as they were moments when he was reassured of the aims of the struggle that he was leading. At those moments, he also condemned the thoughts of limitations that wanted to stop him from achieving his aim and he was able to use his conscious mind to discourage the threats from white people that lingered in his subconscious mind.

Taking a look at the lives of other Black successful icons like Oprah and Ursula who was the CEO of Xerox in 2009, you see that they were women who most times placed high premium on the periods of silence they draw out from their ever busy schedule.

In those instances of silence, they consciously remind themselves of the reason they are at the top and the values they must continue to uphold. They also reflect on their humble beginnings and thereafter make conscious decisions to provide help for the Black community in every measure they are able to muster.

Avoiding Scornful Pride

Anyone who may have been reading this book thus far and thinks that it endorses a scornful pride is sorely wrong.

What is pride and how exactly does it differ from scornful pride?

Pride as defined by the dictionary is the quality of having a sense of one's own worth and self-respect. When we delve deeper into the concept of pride, we see that it has beneficial components and devastating components as well. In this case, scornful pride is when an individual begins to exhibit a disdainful behavior, arrogance and insolence towards another person or a group of people.

White people have mostly been conditioned to exhibit a kind of scornful pride whenever they come in contact with Black people and this is as a result of their history as slave-owners who got free labor from their Black servants. Even though that period of slavery has passed and transitioned into an era where the law seems to be partial in theory, most white people still exhibit that kind of scornful pride that makes them think they are superstars even when they encounter Black superstars.

A good example has been mentioned in the early chapter when I talked about Andy my childhood white friend.

For the sake of emphasis, let me give another example of a kind of scornful pride that was exhibited by Adolf Hitler during the Berlin summer Olympics of 1936.

Prior to the Olympics, Adolf Hitler has always boasted that the German white people were the strongest race on earth. He said that they were the fastest, most innovative and this meant that they were destined to rule the earth. While he kept making his boast, there was a Black American sprinter who went by the name Jesse Owens and he was the fastest man as at that time.

Black people have always dominated the field of sprint and like Usain Bolt and Justin Gatlin of the present day, Jesse Owens was a man who ran very fast and always ended up leading the pack. In the prelude to the Berlin 100 meters race, Adolf Hitler kept boasting that German sprinters would outperform Owens but Owens never replied the boast. Instead, the Black icon redoubled his efforts in training in preparation for the D-day.

When the day of the sprinting came, Adolf Hitler was in the stadium and watched on with the rest of the world as the gunshot indicated the start of the 100 meters race. Like a flash, Jesse Owens took off and glided swiftly in the air as he beat every other competitor by a wide margin to the cheers of the people around the world. When it was time for the laurels to be given, Adolf Hitler was not available and Jesse Owens still went ahead to claim three more gold medals in the Olympics even as Adolf Hitler remained silent.

The idea behind this book is that Black people should recognize that fact that they have a glorious history that is not defined only by the period of slavery. A realization of this fact will enable every Black person to adopt self-respect due to his or her heritage. A healthy dose of self-respect is always going to be needed in the process of becoming an achiever because it would help you shut down self-limiting thoughts that want you to believe that you cannot produce anything good. This self-respect is the pride the book wants you to adopt and not the scornful pride.

You should not use your success as a means of hurting other people because they have not measured up to you. This is because the hallmark of any successful person is the ability to rise above the hatred and offer hope to people who were once enemies.

Take a look at President Barack Obama as an example. Despite the fact that many white people worked tirelessly to ensure that he did not get elected into the White House, he still proved himself to be a president that did not neglect the needs of the white population.

At a period in time when he could have easily led a witch-hunt against members of the Republican Party who engaged in campaigns that were spiteful, he chose not to. Instead, he proved himself to be a President for all classes, which included the Lesbians, Gay and Transgender group, and also a president that attempted to tolerate all religions within the country.

Oprah Winfrey is another Black icon that reached the top of her field and has not decided to spite any class or race with her success. When you take a look at the demographic of her audience, you immediately notice a mixture of Black, Hispanic and white women. There are no discriminations because she is determined to provide value for everybody irrespective of how they may have acted to her at any particular time.

Imagine that incident of racism that she faced when she was outside the country, she could have chosen to immediately buy the entire shares of the company in order to have the pleasure of sacking the sales representative or she could have walked up to the manager to introduce herself in order to get the girl fired. Instead, she did not engage in scornful pride

One negative aspect of scornful pride is that it blinds the people to their faults and the possibilities of becoming better in their activities. Take the example of the Black Wall Street community in Tulsa and their white neighbors.

The white neighbors were so much consumed with scornful pride against the wealthy Black people that their eyes were blinded to the reasons why they remained poor.

Need For Change

We must not be so fixated on our past glories and positive statistics that we fail to notice some values that are disintegrating within our communities; some of these values are

- **Hard work:**

This is a value that has been passed down from the first generation of Black people in Africa who built great civilizations due to their industrious nature.

We have reached where we are because many Black ancestors chose to bring our dreams to reality on a daily basis without stopping. Reverend Martin Luther King had a dream and did not only stop at giving the speech. Instead, he chose to move towards bringing his dreams to reality.

In a certain way, we are losing that industrious nature of ours because some of our youths are embracing the ideology that wealth can be gotten through a quick means. This message is sold in most rap songs which have deviated from the messages of civil rights into sending messages that one can get rich quick through illegal means such as selling drugs.

There is a lot we can do to counteract the content of this kind of message as it serves as a medium to lure Black youths into the petty crimes and criminal gangs. To counteract this rising menace, we can begin to point to youths who are pursuing success in the right way.

We should point to Black youths who are making headlines in the Artificial Intelligence industry,

Black youths who are making waves in the Literal Arts such as poetry, prose and drama,

Black youths who are breaking barriers of technology in Silicon Valley and in the Real Estate management,

Black youths who are increasingly reaching the positions of partners in top Law firms across the entire world,

Black Youths who are organizing and leading humanitarian efforts in countries that are experiencing troubles,

Black youths who are serving their country with pride in various deployments across the world.

These are the examples that we need to point to and then urge the youths in our community to aspire to.

- **Brotherhood and Sisterhood:**

The history of Black people has been the one where Brotherhood and Sisterhood flourished and then reduced at some certain points.

In building the great civilizations in Africa, our Ancestors bonded together and shared resources together and it was this brotherhood that made them reach the greatest heights. After all, it was Black people that built the ancient Egyptian civilization with the Pyramids and other wonders of the ancient world.

It was the spirit of brotherhood and sisterhood that made Black people begin to unite against the slave owners. It was a brotherhood that brought about the legends of people like Nat Turner in Southampton County in August 1831, Gabriel Prosser in Virginia in 1800 among others who led slave rebellions that brought their freedoms.

It was the spirit of brotherhood that drove women like Rosa Parks, and men like Brother Malcolm X during the era of the civil rights movement.

However, one can notice that at the level of our Black communities, the spirit of Brotherhood and sisterhood is gradually ebbing away with the rise of criminal gangs. You can see that most of these criminal gangs espouse values and loyalties to their neighborhoods instead of the entire Black people.

Once again, the hip-hop and rap industry has played a role in fueling this as many rappers pledge allegiance to Westside, Eastside, Bloods, Crips and other gangs.

A true black achiever does not pledge allegiance to any Black group that is intent on bringing death upon other Black people because that would take us back to the era that brought about the slave trade.

This book is challenging every person in gangs to drop their hatred for other Black people in other parts of the community and reunite with the purpose of bringing true development to our communities.

Can you begin to imagine the levels of success that we would experience if we all came together with one purpose of building our community? This should be the true goal of every achiever.

Also, we should begin to ensure that we channel our support towards Black-owned businesses, as this is the only way we can guarantee our growth as a collective.

Black entrepreneurs who are employers of labor, must begin to offer jobs to enterprising Black people and also stop the discrimination against Black ex-convicts. The white man's propaganda is aimed at making everyone believe that every Black person who goes into a prison and returns is not fit to be integrated into the society. This is a lie we have to disbelieve because prisons are meant to be correctional facilities and that means that everyone who leaves should have more opportunities at getting a job and being reintegrated into the society.

As a Black entrepreneur, Black ex-convicts who come to your establishment in search for jobs should not be turned away. Rather, give them the job because it would prove to be a way that they would not return to the life of crime. It should be the responsibility of every Black person to avoid bias because the bias we often have concerning a particular group of persons might end up being the reality.

For example, black women who tend to hold on to the bias that every Black man is always going to cheat in a relationship often find out that their partners cheat irrespective of whatever measures such women take. The reason for this is that such women by their spoken and unspoken words always find means of pushing such men into the act of cheating.

Believing in Yourself

*"It's lack of faith that makes people afraid of meeting challenges',
and I believe in myself."* --Muhammad Ali

There is a popular saying that states that people who do not plan to succeed are already planning to fail. 'Self-Belief' is the component of success that you should begin to plan towards acquiring at every period of your life because it is vital for all Black Achievers.

You either believe in yourself or you don't. There is no better way of explaining that fact. You can either believe in your capability to handle pressure or you believe that you are going to crumble under the weight of challenges. The choice is usually up to you to decide but you ought to understand the way self-belief functions. You need to understand the benefits that you stand to accrue to yourself and your community when you have self-belief.

1. Self-belief inspires everyone around you

Allen Iverson and Kobe Bryant remain two of my most beloved basketball players even as Shaq, Michael Jordan and LeBron James are being mentioned by others.

Have you ever seen Kobe play? You will get so much delight from his pattern of play because you can easily see that he exudes self-belief. When facing opponents in the court, you can see the self-belief in the eyes of Allen Iverson because he KNOWS that he will dribble around them on the path to scoring. Allen Iverson is such a delight to watch because he does not exhibit the slightest fear and this makes other team members play on without showing any fear.

Every team LeBron James plays for always exhibit intense confidence as well because they have LeBron; a superstar who plays with so much belief that he can score from everywhere, block, and begin an offensive that will bring more points.

Every basketball fan can see that the self-belief which players like LeBron exhibit were the major factor that pushed the team towards winning the Championship. As Black achiever, you owe self-belief to yourself and to every Black person around you because it can be the catalyst that spurs them towards achieving great heights.

The story of President Barack Obama's rise to becoming the most powerful man on earth, serves as a mega boost to Black children who will believe in their ability to reach the top. This was possible because Barack Obama chose not to dwell on the limiting factors from his background in his race to becoming the president.

If you are ever going to achieve financial freedom in life, self-belief will be one of the few factors that will attract the necessary team you desire.

For example, if you have a product which you believe will be beneficial to every person engaged in sports, your level of self-belief in yourself will be the greatest factor that would enable you pitch your idea successfully anywhere.

Imagine that you had an opportunity to have a conversation with Oprah about an idea of yours that you want her to invest in. The level of self-belief you have in your product will enable you speak boldly without any trace of doubt and you will stand a high chance of walking out of that meeting with a deal.

Do you know that most boardroom pitches are won as a result of the self-belief exhibited by the person talking? This is because most executives at the roundtable may not pay to much attention to your figures and bogus words: they are looking for that confidence and fire in your eyes and if you are able to show it, you will have your winning moment.

Do not allow lack of self-belief bring about failures for you.

2. Self-Belief opens your eyes to opportunities.

Most Black people remain blinded to opportunities that pass by them daily because they simply do not believe in themselves. In many offices now, many Black people have remained in the same spot for years while other people have progressed because they do not believe that their efforts deserve a promotion.

When you begin to think that you are dispensable, you begin to act in a more reserved way that stifles your creative flow and restricts you from going in to demand promotion.

In most cases I have seen, people who do not really deserve promotion go in to have a talk with the management and emerge with their promotion letters, while at the other hand, those who put in longer hours and provide more value often find themselves stuck and angry with themselves. They will remain stuck at that desk until they realize the need to have self-belief in their capabilities. Having self-belief in their capabilities means they would be able to convince their managers of their ability to handle bigger roles in the firm.

A Black lawyer that has self-belief in his ability to win in the courtroom will automatically begin to reach out to bigger firms who will engage his services because self-belief at most times, translates to success.

The few times that self-belief brings repeated failure is due to the fact that the individual did not build himself/ herself. This is why you have to have something concrete within you before exhibiting self-belief because you will be able to guarantee success when called upon.

Anthony Joshua, the Nigerian boxer who defeated Klitschko, is not your everyday kind of boxer. When you take a quick look at the videos that show his training regime, you will be shocked in a positive way because he trains in a rigorous form. That is the reason why he was able to challenge Klitschko the Ukrainian boxer who held all the heavyweight titles and in the ring, Joshua kept on punching, round by round, until he finally knocked out the great Ukrainian who had dominated the boxing arena for more than seven years and had knocked out heavyweight contenders like Tyson Fury and David Haye.

3. Self-belief opens your eyes to the real you

Many people strut through life by trying to imitate other people and never get to showcase who they truly are. You will have seen them;

- Those who are obsessed with getting a car that is way out of their league

- Those who are hell-bent on owning a home that they cannot afford

- Those who want to 'live it up' but do not have the means in order to do so

I think everyone has met people like these at one particular time in their lives and it is just pathetic to watch them trying to become another person without discovering who they truly are on the inside.

You may see Oprah in her private jet going to the Bahamas on a pleasure weekend and think that your life sucks since you are not doing the same but this is not the way winners think.

Winners and Black Achievers are not striving to live in someone else's world because they are comfortable living in theirs. Imagine if Taraji P. Henson finds herself angry because she wants the kind of life that Maya Angelou had?

Imagine if she spent her early years trying to become a famous poet and struggling woefully because she wants to gain the kind of fame that Maya Angelou has gotten. It would be a perfect waste of talent if she had tried this because no one would have ever seen her acting. At the moment, she is enjoying the same kind of fame that Maya Angelou had and loving her role: that's the kind of success you should aspire to get!

You will never be comfortable living in another person's dream so do not try at all. This because you will be faced with the same challenges that the person is faced with and while you will falter in such challenges, the other person would glide through because they chose that path of life.

Begin to build up a healthy perception of what you are doing at the moment. The dreams that you have are peculiar to you because you have been gifted with the special skill set that will enable you to break through in that line of career.

If you find yourself having the dreams of a showman, you must continue to persist in the belief that you will become the greatest showman on earth and this should drive you every time you engage in your performance. Even though it seems that your neighbor is making some real bucks in his line of work and has begun to live the life you visualized, you should persist in your dream and put more effort into making your brand a global one.

If you have the goal of owning the best pet vet store in the entire world, you should keep on holding on to that dream and give your best towards taking excellent care of every animal that is brought into your store. You can become something like an animal whisperer who seems to get the animals to do everything you want and the truth is that you will be celebrated one day. Good news spreads fast and when people begin to see you at your store, exuding much confidence and self-belief, you will eventually get to sit down with the best in the world.

There is little or no happiness gotten at the top for those who took the pathway of other people. They only become sad at the realization that they would have been much happier if they had simply stuck to their dreams and goals.

Some Black people, who were becoming famous, chose to leave the public scene and pursue quaint careers such as teaching because they really had self-belief in their abilities and loved teaching. While other people may have seen this kind of move as wrong and stupid, those who tried it will live happily into their old age with smiles on their faces and a wonderful life lived.

Like this book has shown you, it is never too late to begin.

- It is never too late to begin to chase your real passion if you have been trying to chase other peoples dreams.

- It is never too late to map out the trajectory which you want your life to move

- It is never too late to redraw and strategize who your mentors are.

The Power of Prophecy

Everyone prophesies: it is just a matter of whether they do it consciously or unconsciously.

Prophecy is the ability to determine the future, and it is also the explicit action of saying how the future would look like. For instance, you are walking down the park with your mates and then the clouds begin to gather. At that instant, almost everyone would conclude that it is going to rain but someone may stand out and say that it will not rain. If it rains in that instance, it does not matter because nature does not listen to the words of a few people who may be joking around. But, the ability of one person to say another thing while the crowd is sticking to one line of reasoning is what is important.

You must learn and internalize the ability to prophesy good things even though everyone around is maintaining looks of gloom.

Lets say you find yourself in a company that has about 10% Black employee and 90% white employees.

Naturally, since the white man is configured to frustrate a Black person from reaching the corridors of power, it would be difficult for the Black employees to reach the topmost positions in the company.

In this scenario, most of the Black employees would not even bother with trying to aspire to reach the top because they would feel that they would certainly not reach the top. Most of such Black employees may show indifference to anyone among them that begins to show an aspiration to reach the top and in some cases, that person may be mocked. However, if you are among that workforce, you should be the one to prophesy positive words that you are going to become the first Black person to become the CEO.

The reason why you should do this is that it is very important to identify what is often referred to as the 'Herd Mentality' and disassociate yourself from it.

The Herd Mentality is that people generally tend to think in the same way that is popular. In the case of the company we are speaking of, you should believe that you will reach the top.

Prophesying this means that you can immediately begin the process of training yourself to lead when you reach the top.

- It means that you may begin to take night classes on the best managerial skills

- It means you will begin to read books on power and how to speak persuasively

- It means you will conduct broad-based research into the company's history and then begin to focus on the best way you can improve the company in its niche

- It means you will begin to volunteer to perform the 'dirty' jobs that no other employee would be enthusiastic to take.

Now, be rest assured that while you are engaging in this, other employees may become restless and still continue to discourage you with their negative prophecies. They would bring up some kind of depressing statistic to show you the need to slow your roll and act like them and unfortunately, some of those people may be Black people as well.

Do not be alarmed that they are saying so because they have been conditioned like we have mentioned from the beginning of this book. Such people's mindset has been totally brainwashed to think that even though they do excellent things, they would never break through the ranks of the White system.

Let us return back to you.

The beautiful thing about life is that opportunities pass by us at the faintest time that only those who are ready grab ahold of it and move away. While you are engaging in the activities and still prophesying positively, a slot WILL DEFINITELY open up within the company.

The word Will combined with Definitely are both definite articles which have been used to describe things that happens on a 100% basis. So let me reiterate that statement again;

While you are engaging in the activities and still prophesying positively, a slot WILL DEFINITELY open up within the company

This open slot may come in different forms. It may come in the CEO's sudden decision to try out new managers. It may arise out of the Boards decision to suspend a rogue manager and appoint a temporary one. It may arise when a manager dies during an important phase of the company and there is no time to hire a new manager. It may even arise out of a new Government policy that states that the Black Employees should be given a quota at the decision-making table.

At the point when such an opportunity opens up, who do you think the company would easily look to fill the position? You, of course.

It would not matter that some White people will think that you are too ambitious because every company is always geared towards making profit, and if they recognize that you are a sure banker that can bring that profit, they would have no other option but to promote you to the position.

Once you are in your new position, you should never rest your oars or give any room for slackness. Rather, you must keep honing your skills and sharpening your resume with good prophesy coming out of you.

Fortunately, that visitor called 'opportunity' is a great gorgeous lady that comes around every time and when she comes again, another slot will open and guess who will be picked amidst the grunts from other white people, You!

Handling Criticism

Nobody likes to get a negative feedback. Not even you! We all love to revel in the undulation and the accolades which people shower on us, and when our ears begin to detect a sound of criticism, we race into our hard shells.

The truth, however, is that Black Achievers are never afraid of criticism. As a matter of fact, most successful people actually pay people huge sums to criticize their inventions or policy decisions.

Let us take the case of celebrated Black Literary figure Maya Angelou for example. Every great poet and prose writer understands that in order for a book to be regarded as a masterpiece, it must go through the scrutinizing hands of beta readers and then an editor who would usually tear the work into figurative shreds and then urge the writer to reconstruct it better.

Now, while this may sound like a disaster waiting to happen to the mental state of budding writers, the experienced writers always look forward to this stage of their work because it is a stage where their works leave the stage of ordinary to extraordinary.

Kids are most times taught that their little creations are awesome and this kind of complements boosts their self-esteem but creates little challenge in the future. When they grow up and create the same kind of stuff, they immediately expect praise like before but when they get criticism instead, they become very sad.

In the cases of the experienced writers, while writing and pouring their hearts into the paper, they envision themselves to be creating masterpieces. However, when they give their works to their editors, such editor may point out glaring mistakes in their plot lines and then urge them to create other side stories to make the story flow. The end product of such editing process is that the book ends up winning bestselling awards and the author may later translate into a Nobel Laureate winner.

Every Black person who aspires to become an achiever must never hide from people who criticize him or her because it is only through that process that they become better. At the onset of your career, such criticism may be really damaging to your self-confidence, but you must take it to be a necessary stop sign that indicates danger ahead if you keep on exhibiting the same kind of attitude that people are criticizing.

There is another important thing that you should know about criticism.

You should consciously choose those people who you will listen to.

Everybody has an opinion about everything but not everybody's opinion counts. Imagine if a doctor tries to offer criticism concerning the way Oprah engages her audience? Oprah would not bat an eyelid to the opinion because the doctor absolutely has no experience in hosting a Talk-show while she has a lot of experience in that area. However, if Steve Harvey decides to extend criticism to Oprah, she would listen because he has experience in hosting Talk shows as well and could be offering something that is actually beneficial to her.

You cannot be into a line of work and then listen to everybody's opinion. Politely offer your 'thank you' response to those who have no idea about what it means to be in your line of business and then focus on improving on the criticism you get from those who have more experience or are into the same line with you.

Understand that some people may be genuinely concerned but still offer useless criticism. Also, make it a point of duty to leave the place where praise singers are in order to listen to the voice of those who are blunt.

Untangle your mind and listen

Often, your mind will try to prove itself right in the line of action it is taken and you will wish to ride against the storm of criticism. Do yourself and your precious time a big favor by choosing to listen to seasoned professionals and then going on to make an informed decision to either continue in your path or stop.

Law of Attraction

The law of attraction simply states; You attract whatever you think about, good or bad. It does not matter if you believe in the power of the universe or any other thing: the fact remains that positive thinking is very potent in its application. The underlying idea is that Like attracts Like.

Attraction of good and bad experiences based on thought

There is a wealth of research that proves that people who believe they would get sick with a certain illness often end up having such illness. The same thing applies to everyone who speaks more about prosperity. The disposition of the human mind towards a thing always attracts it or repels it.

By the simple act of thinking of a scholarship and focusing too much on it, you would realize that scholarship opportunities would begin to showcase it more than others who are not thinking of it.

Immediately a human being affixes the mind on a pattern of thinking, the thinking goes deeper and then mind barriers that shield that thing are broken into pieces. In some occasions, the church urges people to have faith as a prerequisite to getting a miracle and the reason is that the person's mind must be set on scaling over the hurdle that lies before them.

Trusting your emotions instead of overthinking

The simple thing to be understood here is that you should always learn to go with your intuition. In most occasions, overthinking a choice means that you may begin to visualize the negative aspects of what you desire and this begins to flood you with feelings of loss and thoughts of giving up.

To combat these feelings of loss, it is pertinent that we choose to channel positive emotions towards the thought so that we would continue to attract the success we desire to achieve.

To make change happen, see things as you hope and not the way they are

The biblical description of faith is that it is the substance of things hoped for but not seen yet. This is the only description that is best for hope because every journey embarked on must have a destination in mind.

Being successful will require you to always believe in the picture of a richer you in the future because this picture is going to be the motivating factor that will help you stay afloat when the challenges come.

Are you aspiring to become the richest person in your field? You have to keep believing that things are going to be better and this means you must always have a positive disposition that sees optimism when other people around you are seeing a downturn. This optimism will be a magnetic field that draws success closer.

In order to adopt this level of optimism, spend about 15 minutes everyday meditating on your goals and dreams.

Success is not a finite resource; there is available access to everyone

Remember what I said about the social conditioning that the White man engages in, in order to keep you down? Part of such brainwashing is that He wants you to think that the roads to success can only be filled with White people and that no Black person is worthy to walk within.

You should reject this lie by making your research to discover countless Black people who are making real progress in their respective fields. This automatically means that you are not restricted from attaining your own success and it is important that you try and make sure you support other Black people in their bid to become successful. Teach your children that the sky is big enough for all birds to fly without colliding against each other and in the same way, every Black person can become successful.

Disappointment is a pit you must not remain inside

It is true that Black people may have had a past that has not been savory but that should not be your focus. Our ancestors in Africa built great civilizations that were the first and this should serve as a source of pride for you. The same applies to you today because you should never dwell long on a disappointing experience in your journey to the top

Understand that you have bad relationships because we created them

Since the law of attraction states that good attracts good, it means that every time you spend giving attention to the negative things about someone would make the relationship worse. In your personal relationship, develop a positive mentality about the other person and about your neighbors so that you can be able to build a hitch-free relationship.

One beneficial aspect about seeing positives is that when a negative experience happens, you will easily forgive and then continue to build a better relationship with the person.

Always ask the positive 'What if'

Your mood is usually the most important aspect about you that you must treasure because if your mood is always negative with thoughts of gloom, you will not be able to attract success at all.

To counter this, always ask positive questions that would help improve your mood and make you look on to the bright side of every situation.

Here are some positive 'What if' questions to help you:

- What if things work out the way I want

- What if things are like this because they are pointers to my close-by success

- What if it is just a temporary setback and not a total loss

- What if I go home and rest with the knowledge that things will work out later

- What if I am the fantasy of that beautiful lady I am scared to approach

- What if I get that money in a way that is shocking to me

Self-Motivation

Every choice made consciously or otherwise has the ability to either motivate us or decrease our self-esteem. Even though we need to know where we are going beforehand in terms of visualization, there is a need for self-motivation that often demands more than we think. In a bid to utilize the Law of Attraction with the power of self-motivation, there is a certain course of action that must be taken.

Black people who often sit and come up with goals that have no actions are victims of a terrible daydream. Your dream can only come into life when you master the tools of motivating yourself.

Create a Vision

Vision creation is the process where you decide who you want to be in the future after which you can then begin to work your real self into that portrait. In this way, you are actively determining who you will be and this will seem like someone living in fantasyland.

However, every great invention began in the realm of fantasyland until it began to come into reality in bits. This book dares you to challenge yourself and your children to think as this will make you break through the stereotypes and show the White man your superiority once more.

Break free out of your comfort zone in this vision creation process so that you do not re-do what another person has done. Rather, think totally outside the box with an energetic effort put into every thought.

There is absolutely nothing that can stop you when you decide to move out of sorrow and disappointment by the three action words, GO. DO. MOVE. As the course continues to advance, you will also need to check your progress and measuring it with that visual image which you have set in your mind from the start of the journey.

Clearly Define your Goals

People who traditionally set very small goals often end up being disillusioned at the end because such goals are unable to spur them at every point. For example, a hiker who only plans on reaching the peak of a small mountain may not experience true happiness when she discovers that other hikers are gunning for the peak of Mount Kilimanjaro.

The idea is that you should aim for goals that will continue to excite your imagination till the end of your life when ultimately you will be joyful that you have lived a purposeful life.

In defining your goals, you should make sure that they are not too much so that you do not end up chasing many things without getting any of them done. To do this, you must be able to identify your body chemistry, understand your likes and then fashion your goals in a way that you can fully focus on them. The benefit of clearly defining your goals is that you will not easily tire and it would be easy to keep feeding yourself with the needed positive motivation that is needed.

Have fun along the way

Kids are a delight to watch when they are playing a sport they are enjoying. While it is being played, they may encounter falls and timeouts but they are not deterred from going on because they are having fun all along the way.

Remember my 11-year-old experience when I was playing with Andy? I was beating him and other teammates because I was really having fun in the games. The same should happen for you as you strive to achieve your goals. Do not design your life based on what other people think because you will obviously come short at every turn and there would be no true fun.

Having fun along the way means that you are not fazed with the downturns that will come your way. It means you do not care what the media says the Black Community and you are not really fazed by the negative stereotypes that people have because you are assured that you will overcome every challenge that comes your way.

Do not judge yourself during the process of chasing your goals. Instead, keep asking the 'What If' set of questions that are going to give you positive feelings. Ensure that you give your goals everything that is within you while ensuring that you remain kind to Black people who may require your help.

At this point, I want you to turn off every appliance and Internet connection that may be limiting you from focusing on what is needed. Turn off every program that is trying to sell you negative stereotypes about the Black people.

The reason why you should turn off the media is that it is usually filled with the lives of other people who are achieving their goals while yours remain stagnant. It is just like paying to watch your neighbors mow their lawns while weeds continue to infest yours.

Take a couple of minutes to take deep introspection into your progress in order to discover if you are truly happy or you are just acting the script which other people have crafted out for you.

Be Strategic in Accomplishing Your Goals

There is this riddle that keeps making the rounds and it goes like this, How do you eat an elephant? The immediate thought that comes to your mind is that you cannot eat it whole; hence the best way to eat it is to cut it into smaller chunks.

Being strategic means breaking down your work, goals and tasks into smaller portions that are easier to achieve.

Being strategic also, in a way, means that you should make provision for laziness at the onset because you cannot remain motivated from start to the finish line.

Understand the principle of starting small and then finishing big because every big business started from scratch. Starting small will help you avoid the mistake of jumping early into big risks because such risks may likely spell the end of your goals.

Being strategic means you will have to leave every negative acquaintance behind while walking away. It is never easy to leave those you have known for a long time but because you have a goal that you have to achieve within a set time, a polite parting would have to occur.

Possibility often vaporizes in an environment of stagnancy and cynicism.

Recognize the fact that you are a genius whose mind is capable of creating anything positive. This means that your mind has the capacity of creating the best-case scenario as well as the worst-case scenario. Why would you settle for the latter when you could go for the former? White superiority would want you to always think of Black people as naturally inclined towards average but this is not true.

Choose to maintain a positive outlook on any position you find yourself in the course of reaching your goals. Happiness is not necessarily the end product of a goal because it can be gotten during the process. The process of associating happiness with what is not present will deny you of the power of creating it yourself.

Develop the boldness to race towards your fear

This is because the best gift is waiting for you at the other side of fear that you are scared to cross. Working gradually through the fear will build a high level of self-confidence in you that would be useful in helping you face higher challenges.

A popular quip states that Death only strikes viciously once but fear strikes many times and renders many dreams lifeless. A quick way you can overcome the insurmountable fear is for you to always address the most difficult task on your hands first. When you solve this, every other thing becomes relatively easy.

Create Beneficial Relationships

Your full potential is only ever actualized when you work in tandem with other people, as there are no mind-blowing projects that came to existence out of a solo person. Every individual on earth was created like angels having one wing and that is the reason why we need one another to enable ourselves fly.

Every Black person that aims to truly be great should be ready to internalize the principles of collaboration because we are often at our brilliant best when we begin to work with others.

At a point in your live, you may need the help of a superman or a superwoman who would swoop in and save your bad day. Such supermen do not magically come into play; you will need to build relationships with people based on providing value for them before they can also provide value for you when you need help.

The White man's propaganda machine will want us to believe that Black people are terrible at collaborations and only come together when we want to engage in terrible harm but this is not correct at all. When you begin to take up the responsibility of creating a great relationship based on mutual respect for each other's goals and dreams, collaborations become easier.

However, you will not need to collaborate with everyone because some people are not towing the line of industry that you are on and some may not have the same passion as you. That is why you would have to be disciplined to say no to other negative relationships while maintaining a positive feeling. You should realize that you might be hurt during the process of building a beneficial relationship.

However, you should remember that you will have to tolerate people's faults while also teaching your kids to learn the art of toleration so they do not easily end any beneficial relationship that they may be into.

Deprogramming Yourself

Remember everything we have been saying about propaganda? You will need to bring it to bare here. One way you easily de-program yourself is building the ability to spot a lie from afar.

The quality of spotting a lie is built when you begin to read books like this that tells you about the greatness of the Black Race. There are agendas put in place by the White man to bring you down psychologically and make you feel like a failure all the time. Once you detect these agendas, smile and shut them away while moving towards your dreams.

Practice the art of being alert and grounded in the present while looking hopefully to the future.

Do not ever make the mistake of staying in a place and moping about your past because it will not change. You can do something about it by picking yourself up and channeling your focus towards productive activities.

Stay motivated by increasing the money flow

Nobody can ever get enough of money, as the human wants are always insatiable. This is one of the reasons why you should strive to be financially well to do so that your compassion for others can be fueled with the ability to meet their needs. Do not buy into the White man's belief that you would have to cheat others to make money as a Black person. Rather, you can make money the noble way that is being taught in this book and then use the money to shower love and attention on those who are in desperate need of it.

Ask questions

Always learn to ask questions within your relationship because it helps you to understand what is happening per time while ensuring that your power vision is being created.

Motivating others

A fascinating fact about Black people is that we always come together to support our own with words of encouragement and we stand as one against the oppressors. We have to keep up this tradition by making sure that we motivate people even if we really need to be motivated. The benefit of this practice is that you can get inspiration whenever you motivate other people else to achieve their goals

Hold an engaging conversation with yourself

Listen well! There is no better way to motivate you than hearing yourself speak to yourself. There is a great power that comes with words and that is why the world came into existence as a result of words. The White superiority has tried to keep Blacks silent for a long time now.

They have tried to silence Black-owned media from giving information about ourselves because it will be difficult for them to stop us when our media tells us our true potential. However, before the media does this for you, you ought to address yourself in self-affirmative words.

You need to stand before a mirror and keep repeating words that approve your self-worth. The same line of action should be extended to our children and our neighbors because like I said, success is not finite.

Speak words that build the self-confidence of that neighbor of yours who is going through a bad time.

Step into your kid's room at odd times and just remind them of their kingly heritage that cannot be taken away from them.

Remind yourself that you are not a spectator who came to watch White people get all the successes. Rather, you are capable competitor and you ought to be making headways. When you are down with self-doubt, remind yourself that you are not a product of a people who are mentally backward but a proud child of a race of powerful people. Always think yourself a perfect being made in Gods image.

If you are into yoga and meditation, you will be able to engage in these words of affirmation better. But, if you are not into yoga and meditation, the power of positive confession still works as you go everywhere.

Live each day as if it were your last

Today is the best day of your life. Not yesterday because that is in past tense and certainly not tomorrow because that is in the future.

Your 'today' is the best moment of your life that you should not only cherish but strive to make better.

The beauty of each day is that it affords us seconds to right the mistakes of the past, minutes to chart an excellent course for the future, and hours to appreciate the beauty of life.

Problems are not exclusive to you so do not act as if they are killing you. This is because you may tend to dwell solely on your problems to an extent that the day passes by without any concrete action done about them.

Answer this, does a sailor sit in his cabin thinking about the storms of the previous night while his cabin enjoys the dawn of the new day? The answer is an emphatic No! Because the storms are gone with the day before.

Do not allow yourself to be restrained by the chains of the past. If you are a Black Father who underwent a scenario wherein your father left as a child, shrug off that past history and make every effort to be available for your kids because you are a King and not a 'dead-beat' like the White controlled media will want to paint you.

If you experienced a terrible loss in your business that seems like it cannot be recovered, you have to consciously make the effort to stop reliving the moments before the loss. The reason is that there is no need beating a dead horse and the only way forward is to live in the moment. Pick yourself up, dust away the tears and the heavy heart and then put on your game face. Go to the section on Leveraging in this book and get the vital information needed in getting back to your feet financially.

Living in the moment is key. It is not just applicable to those seeking business excellence but it is important for family building. I know you have seen those fathers who go to their children's recitals and their heads are bowed over their phones while texting work.

Do not be like those fathers; rather, ensure that you treasure every moment spent with your family because they are watching and they know if you are either faking it or being real with your presence.

Think 'outside the box'

Most human beings tend to have a particular way they view the world and this makes them stay in the same level of success. Black people are kings and Queens and that means that they are not meant to think in the same way. Every challenge is unique and peculiar to everyone but the reason why some people have scaled them while others did not is because they chose to see the problems differently and also chose to think of unique answers.

The white man's propaganda is aimed at making you think that you are not meant to think up ideas that will benefit humanity. This is why they hardly broadcast news stories of Black people who are innovators that created tools that saves lives or makes things work better. Instead, they choose to broadcast news of violence in Black communities and are especially delighted to broadcast news of the failings of some Black people just like Mike Tyson, Tiger Woods etc.

All this propaganda is a lie meant to keep you from recognizing your true potential because in reality, Black people are one of the greatest inventors ever. Black people like Maya Angelou, Malcolm X, Wole Soyinka, Chimamanda Adichie are the leading figures in the field of the literary arts.

Black people like the three Black women scientists who designed the rocket spaceship that landed the first man on the moon. These are stories of highly successful Black people and most especially, stories of Black people who made it a point of duty to think outside the box.

You cannot operate in the same mental capacity like other people if you desire success. Success requires you to adopt a radical mindset towards challenges and it requires you to condition your mind to always think of 'other' options.

The concept of 'other' options is that when you are exhausted with listing the traditional ways of scaling a problem, you begin to list the 'untraditional' ways that other people would not consider.

It means as a Black person seeking financial freedom, you should research the unexplored industries where you can break into and carve a niche for yourself.

Who says Black people cannot break into the Artificial Intelligence industry and dominate?

What is going to stop you from becoming a Formula One driver who would smash the thinking that it is a white man's sport?

Who says that we cannot establish the highest employing startup in Silicon Valley?

These questions are meant to spur you towards thinking outside the box. Understand that there is no 'white-dominated sport or industry' as the media would want you to believe. There are only places where Black people are yet to explore because when we do explore those areas, we immediately dominate.

It is vital that you teach your kids the need to think outside the box because you will be building a generation of children who dare to go anywhere and are not afraid to test any innovation. Teach them that they would have to distance themselves from some of their friends because the magnitude of their ideas would shock such friends.

Nevertheless, even though they eventually build the biggest startup in Silicon Valley, remind them that Black people are not crabs and employing Black people within the company will not bring the company to ruin. That is another stereotype that the white man wants every Black person to believe.

Silence that Voice called "Negativity'

There is an unfortunate line of action that we take as humankind and that is negative thinking. In most occasions, the question that comes to your mind when you want to take a big leap into success is, 'What if I don't succeed?'

Of course, the road to success is known as the 'risk road' and it is a lonely road because most people see the name and immediately make up their minds not to take the road. This book has taught you that financial freedom will be gotten when you get a passive stream of income where you can retire early but there is a high amount of risk that is involved when you want to begin taking that path to financial freedom.

Your mind will fight against you in a way because it would be subjected to a higher level of thinking than it was accustomed to.

Your friends will subtly fight against you in a way because the process of building your empire will require you to leave them for longer stretches of time and also require you to get a newer set of friends who will become your network.

In most occasions, your family may fight back in a subtle way because you would no longer spend much time with them while monies will be channeled more towards the business you are building.

Finally, the system will fight you very hard because it is being controlled by the white man whose propaganda is still thick. The system may fight you through the banks, the authorities and even through other Blacks nevertheless, you must retain your positivity even in the face of all these negativity.

You will constantly be in a mental courtroom where you will be the judge and negativity will attempt to disrupt your court. Every time, negativity raises an 'objection' and lists various reasons why your intended course of action will not work, you should consciously shut down the interruption and continue with your course of action as if you were never interrupted. There is absolutely no harm in trying because you are embracing a possibility of success but there is great harm in not trying at all because you are choosing to ignore the possibility of success.

When negativity comes like a deluge, try a game of brainstorming. In this game, pick up your pen and then write out 20 ideas that can help you overcome the present challenge you are faced with. If you are feeling as if you are never going to be successful in life, let us try the game of brainstorming as well. In the game, write out 20 strengths that you know you have and then write out twenty business ideas which you thought of. No idea is ever silly so just keep writing and don't cancel.

At the end of the writing exercise, begin to match the strengths with the ideas you wrote down and if you feel as though you are having challenges with this cross-matching, take the paper and go and meet a business friend who would show you that you are not a failure because you have an innovative mind.

Apply force

There is a law propounded by Isaac Newton that is the second law of thermodynamics. This law is the law of Inertia and it basically states that an object will remain in inertia until force is applied. The state of Inertia is the state of being motionless.

A typical example of something that is inertia is a swimming pool or any body of water that is not being fed by any other water source.

Inertia is a state where nothing is moving: a physical state of silence and no action in motion. This is the worst state that anyone can ever be because it means that the person remains stagnated like a lifeless statue condemned to remain in a certain spot for all humanity.

Even as you are reading this book, you will have to apply force to your pursuit of success by undertaking the exercises within the book and not viewing it as another leisure reading.

You will need to apply force on your brain by making yourself engage in deeper research concerning financial opportunities.

You will have to apply force on your character by not retaliating against any word that is spoken against you by your business partner because you still desire to salvage that business deal.

You will have to apply force on yourself by standing up and walking out on films that do not paint correct stories of the Black experience even though your favorite actors are the ones that starred in the film.

Nothing ever gets done in a society where there is no action. The civil rights movement would not have achieved the successes against the white man's system if everyone had chosen to stay home when the marches were called. Our ancestors back in Africa would not have built magnificent civilizations if they had just folded their hands and stood around all day.

Let me digress a little bit to show you the extent to which our African ancestors were industrious;

Many historical accounts and sources such as Tarikh and many textbooks tell of the great civilizations of Mali and Songhai Empire. They both were very popular for producing great leaders who thought of great means of improving their empire while they also experienced increased expansion.

One of the leaders was known as Mansa Musa. After ascending the throne, Mansa Musa decided to travel to the Middle East in a bid to building a blossoming relationship with other Kings. It was recorded that Mansa Musa owned many camels and helpers but the particular fact that struck many writers was the riches that were exhibited by him.

All his camels, which were in their thousands, were loaded with gold and everything he wore along with his assistants were crafted in pure gold. It was recorded that at every village Mansa Musa stopped, he gave out gold bars to the poor people and built edifices that bore his insignia.

All these, and many more charitable acts as well as a display of wealth was performed by our Ancestors without any help from white people. As a matter of fact, no white man had arrived in the African continent at the time that Mansa Musa was king and all his deeds had been recorded by Arab Historians and white Historians who were in the Middle East at that time.

The idea Black people should get from this account is that there is nothing that can stop them if only they apply force to their dreams which are still in a state of inertia.

 Perhaps one of the ways that you can come out of that state of inertia is when you adopt some rituals which would enable you to jumpstart the force you need. Some of such rituals have already been stated like the game of brainstorming as well as the constant repetition of positive affirmations that would help build your confidence

Change comes in Trickles

They often say that the journey of a thousand miles begins with a step. The meaning implicit within that popular saying is that everyone who intends to embark on any mission or task must adopt the virtue called Patience.

According to the dictionary, patience is the uncomplaining endurance that anyone must undertake during the course of anything. Being humans, patience has never really been a virtue that we idolize and this is visible in the emerging technologies that rule our world patiently.

Humans do not want to be patient in building meaningful friendships through physical meeting and discussions and that is why they built social media applications like Facebook so people can easily become 'friends' and then proceed to 'liking' everything about their new friends.

New dating websites where people go straight to sex talk keeps coming up because people are not willing to endure the process of meeting themselves for the first time, discussing to share their passions and then move on toward getting to share a more intimate bond.

We are so desperate these days that we have applications for almost everything; from shopping within our homes to booking our personal flights across the world. This age of frenzy is causing a problem that is not very pronounced, and it is creating a brick wall for many people chasing success.

The problem that is being created is that anything slow is seen as 'not good'. Any connection that is slow is 'not good' and every car is priced higher if they are seen as speeding beasts on the roads.

Unfortunately, the process of building your business or achieving any form of success takes time.

This means that it takes a painstakingly slow process that requires you to have a positive mentality throughout the process. In the case of most people, they will never make it through the early stages of success because they get irritated when the process is not fast.

Let us take for example the spouses of war veterans. In most cases, the spouses of war veterans end up suing for a divorce from their partners who have just returned from war because of the prolonged case of Post-Traumatic Stress Disorder.

Doctors who treat such cases always state that it is a condition that would take a while to heal since most of such sufferers were exposed to the horrors of war. It will take you time to build a successful relationship with your spouse.

Yes. Emotions are fleeting in nature and it takes serious work to stir the love within your partner.

In the case of men, it would take more than sending a dozen red roses every day to her doorstep with perfumed cards that bear heart-moving poetry. You would actually have to stay with her during those moments she wants to talk and 'actually listen' with the aim of contributing.

For the women, it would take more than the incredibly sexy gowns to make him continue to love you. You would have to understand the concept of boundaries and also learn to trust in him without always listening to the things your girlfriend or the society says about Black men in general. Unfortunately, the propaganda of the white man has spread and keeps conditioning most Black women to believe that Black men are prone to irresponsibility whenever they are not around their partners.

For Black parents, in acquiring success in terms of rebuilding broken bridges with your kids, you must understand that patience is one virtue that you cannot do without because you will be frustrated and will need that patience to remain calm.

You see, the white man has engaged in a campaign of propaganda that paints all Black parents, especially the fathers, as an irresponsible set of people who are more interested in engaging in drugs, robbery and other nefarious crimes more than staying home to take care of their kids. The problem with this stereotype is that it conditions most Black kids to see their fathers as 'no-gooders' who should not be allowed into their lives or praised for their attempts at providing for the family.

It is a quite unfortunate trend but there is a light at the end of the tunnel for fathers who have kids who think this way.

Patience is the virtue you should have so that even though your kids begin to throw tantrums, you will be patient enough to help them through the process of accepting you. The benefit of the process is that the stereotypes would be discarded and Black kids will recognize that their fathers indeed love them.

This book will talk on principles of Acquiring wealth as a road to Financial freedom later on but let me just chip this in at this stage. In working with your business partner or your boss at work, you will need to adopt the virtue of patience because you cannot keep yelling and then expect promotion to arrive. At some point, your business partner would attempt to seek clarifications on certain aspects of your relationship or try to correct you and if you are not patient, you may explode and ruin the relationship that is needed to push you towards reaching financial independence.

I have observed most people fail in businesses and given the boot from their workplaces because of their lack of patience that hampered their relationship. The self-introspection examination I want you to perform as you read this book is to ask yourself how patient are you?

Build Wealth

Step 1: Develop a Wealthy Mindset

There is nothing better than having a wealthy mindset, as it is the foundational tool for building wealth. The things that your mind believes about wealth are the exact things that will happen to you and that means that skepticism about wealth brings no wealth at all.

How can you then cultivate a wealthy mindset?

The answer to that question lies in your level of decision making accompanied by your level of dogged persistence in what you believe in. Those who believe they would become wealthy, begin to envision themselves swimming in riches. And from there, they begin to step out of their comfort zone. Your comfort zone may represent that place that you have become used to and the kind of decisions you have been making. Those comfort zones must be left and you must exercise commitment and decisiveness in your decision-making.

Once your foot is on the pedal towards becoming rich, you should ensure that you never take it off the gas to slow down for anything or give up. The reason why the graveyard is filled with many riches is that most of them either stopped midway in becoming rich or never attempted reaching for the stars. You should know that you would be drawn towards losing your faith in your dreams at a particular point in your journey because success is not going to automatically align itself on your path. Even though you encounter failures, brace yourself and fight till you reach the top.

STEP 2. Build a Nest Egg

Every bird begins to build a nesting place when she is ready to give birth to her young and you should begin to plan towards your destination. How much wealth are you aspiring to get? How much value do you intend to provide? And you should endeavor to know how you intend starting your nesting place either by accumulating capital or borrowing to start off

STEP 3. Find a Mentor

It is very vital that you realize the essence of getting mentors in building wealth; this is one of the secrets that will give you an inroad into achieving wealth faster.

Let us paint this scenario of you traveling to a country like Egypt in Africa. When you reach Egypt, you would immediately be confronted with the Arabic language that you may find very difficult to comprehend. Now, let us say you find yourself a translator who then begins to take you to different parts of Cairo that you wanted to visit while also helping you pick out the best meal that is good for you. In that way, the translator has made life easier for you.

The same thing is applicable in terms of a mentor. The mentor helps to guide you from becoming totally lost and the person helps you shorten the time for learning. Go and get a Black person as a mentor who can teach you on the way he or she reached the top of their field. Even if it means that you will have to read their books and follow them on social media, ensure you do so as it will be beneficial to you.

Strategies for Wealth Acquisition

I want to introduce you to the proven ways that you can take towards building sustainable wealth that would improve your standard of living.

1. Finding a mentor and enlarge your network

The first strategy is that you should begin to change your environment in terms of the friends you keep. Wealthy people often associate with themselves because of the opportunities they get to share with themselves. You should begin to make a concerted effort at building a network of goal-driven individuals along with getting a mentor that can teach you the rudiments of whatever action you intend taking. You can join Black Achievers (www.BlackAchievers.com) and instantly add thousands of people to your network.

2. Get paid what you are worth

As an employee, there is nothing more depressing than remaining in the same level of pay when others are getting more. This is the reason why you should strive to advance yourself on a personal basis and then begin to strive towards getting the jobs that will bring in the big bucks. If you intend to remain in the same industry, why not walk up to the boss, White or Black, and politely request to be paid as a result of the efforts you have been putting in. You should show no shame when doing this.

3. Reduce your expenses.

You should know that the road to the throne is not always paved in pure gold and the process of cutting your expenses is not easy. Yet, if you want to attain financial freedom, it is one step that you must take.

You can begin by consolidating your long-term debt and start ensuring that you buy your store goods in bulk rather than little quantities. The process of cutting your expenses may also require you to budget more strictly with emphasis on reducing late fees, bounced check fees and other fees which are detrimental to your savings. Ensure that you live on 70% or less of your income, invest more than 15% and then 15% should be allotted to reduction of debts. You can do it!

4. Reducing your Consumer debt

It is always difficult for people living in debt to attain any form of financial freedom as their income is always pumped towards paying off more debts. When paying off 20-30% of credit card debts, you can be sure that saving will be difficult. This is why you should have fruitful conversations with creditors on the need for them to lower their interest rates when they want to give you credit. To better understand these, try and make use of the Resource section of BaronSeries.com where you can obtain your free credit card report that will help you make better financial decisions.

5. Purchase Home Or Investment Property

Real Estate is the goldmine of the future and if you truly desire to be financially independent, you should consider engaging in research that would get you an inroad into this industry. Make sure you engage in concrete research before you embark upon Real Estate as some people have been bitten by the ills of the industry. Nevertheless, it remains a lucrative source of financial wealth buildup.

6. Own your time

You are born to be a creator of wealth and not to keep working for anyone all the days of your life. This is why you should begin to focus on generating passive income instead of focusing on earned income.

An earned income is the one you get from a job or when you are 'self-employed' and its features are,

- It requires your physical presence

- Time is exchanged for money

- You are taxed in a higher way

- Too much time is needed to nurture it

- The income stream stops when you stop and this is not good during retirement stage

The features of Residual and Passive Income

- Your time is leveraged because you can engage in other things that bring another income stream

- You are guaranteed a repeatable model to aid future wealth building

- Your business is taxed at a lower rate

- You are afforded more freedom

- You have your personal time to work better and you have the assurance of a sweet retirement

- Your wealth continues to grow in retirement and you can pass down such wealth to your generation

When you begin to lower your expenses while investing in assets such as Rental Real Estate, tax liens, dividend paying stocks and corporate bonds, you ensure a steady flow of income generation that is bound to keep flowing and this guarantees you an early retirement. Remember that it is best to begin early.

7. Develop a long-term investment portfolio.

Financial freedom can begin to come to pass at any stage of your life and once you begin to understand the power of compounding, you can also begin to tap into the stream of earning big. You can begin by making use of BaronSeries.com that provides an Investment calculator tool that enables you to discover your investment goals while helping you to chart a savings course. It is important that you invest a sum of money that you can afford to lose and also engage in proper research before pitching your resources within.

8. Begin a business

Every Black person has been gifted with a unique brain by God and within that brain lies the power of idea creation. Look around you and then begin to be creative. In the process of this, you will come up with innovative ideas that can benefit humanity and will ultimately generate good funds for you. Never be too afraid to start up your business if you have the conviction to begin as every booming business began with a step into the unknown would of business building.

9. Understand and Adopt the Principle of Leveraging

On a scale of 1 to 10, how many people's skills and resources have you leveraged on? When you choose to engage in everything by yourself, you end up being a colossal failure because you were not meant to simply be an island on your own. The 'Superman' or 'Superwoman' syndrome is when one person thinks they can do everything without people and it does not end well. You should start leveraging on peoples time, money, networks, credibility and also prepare to offer your personal help in return as those people will also leverage on you.

10. Invest in Yourself

There is no faster way to improving your financial status than improving your financial knowledge. You are already doing that by reading this book but you must seek after more. You should learn how to study models and the focusing techniques that have helped numerous Black tycoons to build magnificent businesses. Do not let the white superiority condition you to depend on you physical strength alone because your mental capacity needs to be improved as well.

Transforming into a Savings Expert

1. Sit down and draw up a budget

There is no way you can put a cart before the horse and there is absolutely no way to build finance when you do not cultivate the act of savings. You should learn that the best way to spend money is when you have actually drawn up a budget for it and then stick to that budget rigidly. This is a very important step in becoming a guru at savings.

2. Set aside part of your paycheck

When your paycheck comes, how much do you keep for your savings? While some may say 10% or 15%, the idea is that you should begin to adopt this principle from a younger age as this would help you build up more. This principle is a no-brainer so ensure that you start without further convincing

3. Take advantage of Free Money

When we talk about free money, we talking about the kind that comes when you did not expect it and those moments are very rare I must confess. Even as they are rare, you should identify such monies. For example, in the occasion that your employer matches your 401(k) plan through the putting of an extra dollar from their pockets as you put in your dollar, you will have saved a huge lot of free money because it would have doubled during the period of payout. You should take advantage of that.

4. Take advantage of the Roth IRA plan at an early stage

The Roth IRA plan is one that bears close semblance with the 401(k) plan in that it is helpful for retirement plans. It remains one account that is invested for you without being taxed. As a younger fellow, you should strive to contribute at least $5,000 to the plan on a yearly basis and if you keep at it for a period of 45 years at an 8% annual growth rate, your portfolio would contain such a staggering amount that you would be shocked. The Roth IRA works perfectly through the principle of Compound Interest in which a bank gives you interest on your IRA.

However, as opposed to the traditional method of paying such interest into your personal account, it is put back into your pool and this means that you keep gaining interests over your interests. The early bird gets the juiciest worm and this is why you should start early and most importantly share this information with people in your neighborhood.

5. Wean yourself off credit and Debit cards

Credit cards are super easy to get and seem to be very important to you but do not buy into the social conditioning of the system. The credit cards are tools meant at ensuring that you adopt very bad financial behaviors since you are encouraged to spend money that is not yours.

Research shows that most people tend to see credit and real cash in different light, and while real cash does not inspire them to spend big, credit cash motivates a kind of irrational spending. Cold cash that is yours feels more real to you and brings real discipline as opposed to the virtual one and that is why you should wean yourself off the virtual money.

6. Save Tax Refunds

It is quite unfortunate that most folks tend to be irrational when the government issues a tax refund at the beginning of the year. At that point, they begin to think of the things they are yet to buy and this discourages any form of savings. You are an enlightened Black person and this is why you should not act on impulse at any point. Make calculated efforts in saving such money that you get as it would help you in the future. Also ensure that you pass on this advice to your children, as it is a gem

7. Change your perspective about savings.

You have heard that popular saying "savings is hard".

In some other occasions, you may have tried to begin saving and then failed in the process because of some factors. Nevertheless, this should not deter you from saving because one challenge that makes savings difficult is that most people want to save big. The idea of saving is that you should save in trickles. This means that if you should think of saving little amounts on a daily, weekly basis instead of the big figure in your mind at the beginning of the exercise. If you have the intent of saving $6,000, begin by breaking it down into daily savings rates that would not be too burdensome on your living expenses.

Invest in your Community

A modicum of ways to Invest where your family are;

Your community does not only comprise of the four corners of your home and lawn where your spouse and kids reside. It is a place that transcends the smaller family unit and embraces your friends, and neighbors in a bond that is long lasting and crucially impactful for each other's lives. It is a ground where your children get to intermingle and create value for the world like God destined them to.

However, the glaring reality of the world now shows that many neighbors do not see themselves as families. It is shocking to note that most of them may go for long stretches of time without seeing each other. They instead share brief flashes of curtsey that is not warm. The narrative needs to change as you need to begin investing seriously within your community through numerous ways which may not include money. When you begin the process, your children will see and it will become a learned behavior as the years roll by.

Support Black-Owned Businesses

Many of us are guilty here as we do not tend to always support black-owned businesses. However, you must change the story and the quickest and simplest form of achieving this is to shop at the local stores, support local startups that show great potential and then contribute to family-owned enterprises through your money rather than spending that same money on huge businesses. It is true that you will need to spend more but it will be beneficial to the community in the long run. Spending about $20 on the merchandise of a Black entrepreneur would go a long way in inspiring them to reach the top of their business, as they would have the flexibility to employ more Blacks. Two Black websites you can use are: www.purchaseblack.com and www.webuyblack.com

Make Charitable Donations

The idea of doing this is that your community needs to encounter growth that can only come when monetary investment is present. This is why you should organize a form of neighborhood garage sale where you get to donate the proceeds to a cause or charity that brings succor for Black people. Begin to engage in the act of sending used clothes to a thrift store in the neighborhood that could help homeless Black people. While doing this, ensure you carry your children along and encourage them to keep the tradition going.

Volunteer with Local Organizations

Churches, Mosques, Schools and other organizations are wonderful places you can start pitching in your help in ensuring that their activities run smoothly. There have also been programs like food banks and afterschool programs wherein your funding is needed alongside your volunteering. The benefit of engaging in these kinds of volunteering with your family is that you get to build quality networking relationships with others while the seeds of charity are being instilled in your children.

Support Elderly Neighbors

Apart from supporting your community institutions, it is very needful that you begin to identify with the people on a personal level and meet their needs better. In this case, you can begin to ensure that your children recognize the need for helping elderly people with their grueling chores like gardening or shoveling a snowy sidewalk. With your family, you can decide to help a mobility-challenged community member with difficult home tasks and the benefit is that such people will be immensely grateful while your kids learn the noble art of love.

Build Relationships

There is a saying that advocates the building of bridges and not burning them. In doing this, we get to realize that a sense of togetherness is the main ingredient that binds neighbors together. Excellent neighbors strive to do more for them and they strive to ensure that their children imbibe their relationships as well.

Conclusion

We return back to the fundamental question that drove us at the beginning; Why do some Black people succeed when others stagnate?

Just like we said, the root cause begins from the absence of self-confidence in their Blackness. They remain trapped there until they realize the messages from the White propaganda machine are targeted at keeping them down. A staunch rejection of every learned stereotype about the Black people will help you think differently and more importantly, you will be infused with the boldness to walk into your greatness. A conviction naturally comes with a faithful reading of this book as it propels you to achieving the same kinds of positive results and accolades which people like me have gotten throughout the years.

Get this. Your life will never remain the same after this time! With the right mindset it will seem as if you are being followed around by good luck. Your desires will begin to fall in place and you will not continue to wallow in the same misery of pain, anxieties and worries that continue to plague other people.

You have no other excuse to fail and that is why you cannot blame ignorance. Because limitations are self-imposed, you will break free through your mind and then get to understand the extent of your greatness because you are the expression of God and a King and Queen from the first dominant race on the planet.

The process of discovering ones true self is the first step towards greatness. Nothing sounds simpler yet most people do not have the faintest idea of who they are and what life entails. Like a jigsaw, life is waiting for you to insert your self-realization piece in order to get the best picture. The beauty of this is that a willing person can learn the process

The process of reading this book has revealed that success is not a far-fetched dream that eludes a certain class of people but it can be predicted with absolute certainty. You can walk into every paradise you have ever dreamed about only when you make this book an indispensable part of your life.

Only failures are not moved by anything. Champions are moved by the magnitude of their dreams and that is why you should never get worried as a result of the fear factor. There are no laurels for the fearful. Rather, there is a wealth of riches in the hands of people who recognize the power of the mind. Become like a child now and imagine the riches, power, position etc. when you begin to make it a dream, it begins to come into reality bit by bit. Do not allow the negative stereotypes allow you to stop dreaming as they are meant to keep you underneath the white man forever

A strict observance of the instructions outlined in the book will definitely bring positive results. You will become enlightened and then you will be propelled towards achieving everything you set out to do most especially with my techniques at your beck and call.

The ball is in your court now; You can live a life filled with mediocrity or one that is sweetly filled with success. It is your choice.

Bibliography

This book is the culmination of many different ideas, sources and references. Please visit our website below for an updated bibliography:

www.BlackAchievers.com/bibliography

To join up with Michael "Truth" Moore and his organization of Black Achievers, please visit our website and click the "Join Now" button. Visit: www.BlackAchievers.com